Village '
in
WORCEST

Village Walks
in
WORCESTERSHIRE

David Hinchliffe

COUNTRYSIDE BOOKS
NEWBURY, BERKSHIRE

COUNTRYSIDE BOOKS
3 Catherine Road
Newbury, Berkshire

ISBN 1 85306 487 4

Front cover photograph of Kempsey taken
by Bill Meadows

Designed by Graham Whiteman
Maps and photographs by the author

Produced through MRM Associates Ltd., Reading
Printed byWoolnough Bookbinding Ltd., Irthlingborough

Contents

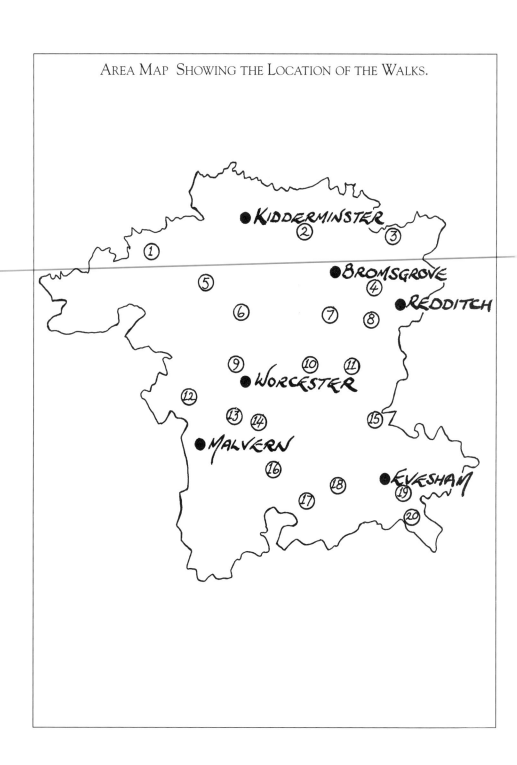

AREA MAP SHOWING THE LOCATION OF THE WALKS.

WALK

❦

Publisher's Note

We hope that you obtain considerable enjoyment from this book; great care has been taken in its preparation. Although at the time of publication all routes followed public rights of way or permitted paths, diversion orders can be made and permissions withdrawn.

We cannot of course be held responsible for such diversion orders and any inaccuracies in the text which result from these or any other changes to the routes nor any damage which might result from walkers trespassing on private property. We are anxious though that all details covering the walks are kept up to date and would therefore welcome information from readers which would be relevant to future editions.

Introduction

I suspect that many people take up walking so as to get out into the countryside, whether that means fields, streams, woodlands, hills or mountains. Villages are a convenient place to park or to buy a few odds and ends. What I have come to realise, however, is that villages are as much part of the countryside as fields or mountains. Most of them grew out of the soil, from farming days, and those that rose in Worcestershire are as pretty as any. So, my aim is to take you out into the countryside, but also to encourage you to explore those villages.

One thing that anyone who walks the routes in this book will soon see is that there is no such thing as a 'typical' Worcestershire village. Nevertheless, the black and white cottage could be the emblem of Worcestershire, particularly when surrounded by blossom laden orchards. Some villages, like Bayton and Wickhamford, at opposite corners of the county, are packed with lovely examples of these ancient structures, but they crop up everywhere.

Near the Cotswolds, half-timbering rubs shoulders with warm honey-coloured stone, as in Childswickham and enviable Elmley Castle. In other places it is red brick which catches the eye. This is particularly noticeable in once-noisy industrial villages, and there is sport in spotting relics of scythe-making in Belbroughton or needle-manufacture in Feckenham. Industry also gave life to the canal age, and the communities which grew up to serve them – walks visit Hopwood and Tardebigge, where the bustle and colour of narrow boats enliven the scene.

A typical village clusters around the village green, and none are more picturesque than estate villages such as Overbury and the Lenches. The ties that bond scattered villages such as Astley and Hanbury are less obvious, but each has its own identity. Often unusual buildings, churches and splendid mansions enrich the experience, and all this before setting foot in what is never less than attractive and often quite beautiful countryside. But there, I'm spoiling the excitement of discovery.

Each walk is accompanied by a sketch map to guide you round the route. However, for those requiring more detail, the relevant Ordnance Survey Landranger 1:50 000 map numbers are also given. To reach the villages, you will probably be taking your car. Car parking locations are indicated in the text, but if they are full, or for some reason unusable, please ensure that you park your vehicle in such a way as not to be a nuisance to those who live close by. Some of the walks commence from the village pub where, it must be stressed, parking is only for patrons. If you intend to leave a car at the pub car park whilst out walking, please consult the landlord first.

Finally, I hope you enjoy the walks, but do allow ample time to explore those unspoilt corners of Worcestershire's wonderful villages.

David Hinchliffe

BAYTON

Length: 4 miles

Getting there: From the A456 6 miles west of Bewdley turn off northwards in Clows Top, and left after about ½ mile for Bayton.	Parking: If you are patronising the inn you may use the car park, otherwise please park courteously on the village street.	Map: OS Landranger 138 Kidderminster and the Wyre Forest area (GR 695732).

There is a feeling of remoteness about life in this north-western corner of the county which belies its easy accessibility. It may then come as something of a surprise to find such a treasure-house of black and white cottages, off the beaten track and surprisingly unadvertised. At one end of the village is the church, commanding beautiful views over the valley of the river Rea and Clee Hill. At the other end the inn sits close to the charming village green. In between are some of the most delectable cottages to be found anywhere in the county, so be an explorer and see for yourself.

The walk takes you from the village

FOOD and DRINK

This may be a quiet area, but there is no lack of choice for refreshments, with the Sun and Slipper and Mamble Craft Centre both catering for exhausted ramblers at the halfway stage. In Bayton itself there is the Wheatsheaf Inn, a lovely country pub which welcomes children and has a very large play area. Home-made specialities include chicken, ham and mushroom pie, and grills are a feature. Vegetarian dishes are also available, but I like to try unusual dishes so prawns Cantonese style (with mangetout, sliced red peppers, onions, julienne carrots and water chestnuts) proved to be irresistible. This is a good place to spend a few days as it also has five letting bedrooms. Telephone: 01299 832262.

green and across quiet, undulating countryside to the village of Mamble. The inn here is the Sun and Slipper, which overlooks the green which harbours its own legend. It is reputed that once a duel was fought here, leaving a bloodstain on the stairs, a stain which can never be removed. The name of the inn originates from the coat of arms of the Lords of the Manor, the Blount family, a sun above a mailed foot – but, as always, there are other explanations. Nearby is the church, unusual in having an attached Roman Catholic chapel. The body of the church is almost entirely 13th century and contains an only slightly more recent effigy of a knight. The tall north-east doorway is now filled in, but was allegedly created to enable a mounted knight to come into the church to be blessed before setting off to the Crusades. Next door is Mamble Craft Centre.

On leaving Mamble you are immediately back into that lovely rolling countryside, before navigating a course through Wissetts Wood. On emerging

there are views of Shakenhurst Hall, a dignified 17th-century house which was refronted in red brick in 1798. An easy stroll to Bayton follows, climbing to the church and those fine views. Finally, the return down the village street is worthy of time to examine those venerable magpie cottages.

THE WALK

❶ Facing the Wheatsheaf Inn go left and then right, down the road signed to Clows Top. As you leave the precincts of the village a footpath sign on the right indicates the path to be followed. The field side is initially on your right, as a stream and a stile are crossed.

❷ At the end of the next field go briefly left along the headland, then right at a waymark post. The stream runs in a little dingle – keep it to your left to find a footbridge. Scramble up the opposite side to a stile and proceed with the hedge now on your left. Ignore a stile to the left but cross one nearby ahead.

❸ Bear half right to a stream. Cross it at a convenient narrowing, unless a bridge has appeared since this book was written. Once over cross a stile in the fence on the right and head up the hill with the hedge

PLACES of INTEREST

Bewdley, an attractive Georgian town on the banks of the river Severn is nearby and from here one can take a ride along the **Severn Valley Railway**. The **Wyre Forest** provides extensive walking opportunities, and there is a visitor centre just off the A456.

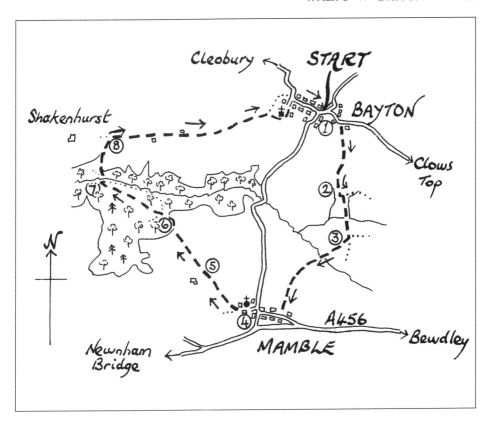

to your left. On the brow of the hill cross two stiles in rapid succession then steer to the bottom left corner of the field. Go over another stile and follow an improving path through a gate and into Mamble. Turn right along the street to arrive at the village green, presided over by the Sun and Slipper.

❹ Take the Bayton road which leads off at the side of the inn, but then immediately turn left down the lane to the church. Just beyond the church is the Craft Centre, but the public footpath runs in front of Tudor Cottage, sandwiched between the garage and a hedge, to come

to a stile. From here bear half right across the field. Pass through a gate in the bottom corner and continue with the field edge on your right.

❺ Cross a track, with Clee Hill in the background. Now bear left of straight ahead to a gate in the far angle of the field. From here continue to head left of the field edge to a stile by the right corner of a wood. Once over follow the edge and shortly enter the wood through a gateway.

❻ The initial path quickly joins a track. Continue ahead to a T-junction. To turn left or right seems obvious, but instead

The village of Mamble visited on the walk.

plunge into the wood, bearing just right of straight ahead. Confidence should be restored by recognition of a grassy track, becoming slightly overgrown, wending its way between the bracken and trees. This track finally descends quite steeply and slipperily to a forestry track.

❼ Go right and immediately left over a stream. The track starts to climb and bend left, but depart from it to the right – the footpath may be faint but the stile at the edge of the wood should be visible. Once over follow the edge of the wood uphill and then bear right to a stile at the top of the field. From here head for the track ahead, with a view on the left of the fine red brick frontage of Shakenhurst Hall.

❽ With your back to Shakenhurst the track soon becomes a minor road. Over to the left is Mawley Hall – the legend is of a dispute between Catholic Mawley and Protestant Shakenhurst. The witch of Mawley put a curse on Shakenhurst so that a son would never inherit the estate. Since that day it has always passed through the female line. At a dip and a footpath sign climb the slope ahead to the church. Sadly the church is usually locked (access details on the door) but this does not prevent an appreciation of the lovely views. Pass through the churchyard and turn left, then right at the junction to walk along the village street to the green.

BELBROUGHTON

Length : 4½ miles

Getting there: From the A491 between junction 4 of the M5 and Hagley turn off on the B4188 for Belbroughton.	**Parking:** On the main street, north of the Talbot pub. If you patronise the Talbot you may use the extensive car park facing the inn.	**Map:** OS Landranger 139 Birmingham and surrounding areas (GR 920771).

Belbroughton is an ancient village, first mentioned in AD 817. Versions of its name have ranged from Broctune to Bryan's Bell. In more recent times it became known internationally as a scythe-making centre. Isaac Nash opened his factory just to the east of the village in 1838, and for a time it was a thriving industry. Eventually, demand declined and Old Father Time called a halt to production in 1968. On the village green you will find a reminder of former glories as a steam hammer is proudly displayed. Older relics include a half-timbered village hall which has seen duty as a tithe barn. The heart of the village is, not surprisingly, found

FOOD and DRINK

Once there were at least eleven inns and alehouses in the village, and thankfully four remain to this day. The spacious proportions and crossroads location of one of these, the Talbot, betray its past as a coaching inn. Here children have their own menu (and goody bags). For grown-ups the menu ranges from starters through steaks to vegetarian dishes and a spicy section. Chicken carbonara, quorn and mushroom lasagne and chicken keema balti supplement the traditional choices. Good beers too – Camerons Strongarm on handpull and Bank's Smoothpour amongst the support. There is an extensive beer garden. Telephone: 01562 730249.

around the village green and the nearby church. Around are cute cottages and the backcloth of the ever-popular Clent Hills.

This walk takes you from the village green to the church, which still possesses a few Norman survivors from the 19th-century restoration. Open country is quickly reached, the route leading by the peaceful pool adjoining 18th-century Drayton House. The tiny hamlet of Drayton sits in an intimate valley, and is left by field paths. Gentle exertion leads to views of the Clent Hills to arrive in due course at the northern extremity of the village. This allows a walk along the village street, crossing the splashing Ram Alley Brook to return to the village green.

A steam hammer proudly displayed on the village green in Belbroughton.

THE WALK

❶ From the village green follow the High Street towards Blakedown and then turn left onto Church Road. Turn right to pass through the churchyard, proceeding along a narrow path at the tower end of the church. This joins a farm track, which is followed to the right. Pass (quickly) by the sewage works. At the bottom of the slope ignore the first path off to the left. The track curves right and on the bend take a faint path leading off to the left.

❷ The path improves, with a wall on the left. Cross the stream and continue left. Go over a stile and Drayton Pool is passed on the left. There is a side view of Drayton House, once the home of Kidderminster carpet barons the Brintons. At the road go left.

❸ Drayton Mill is a pleasant spot, busier in days when it was used for carpet-making, grinding corn and scythe-making. Until 1929 it had the largest water wheel in the country. Turn right along the road signed to Hill Pool and Yieldingtree. Go

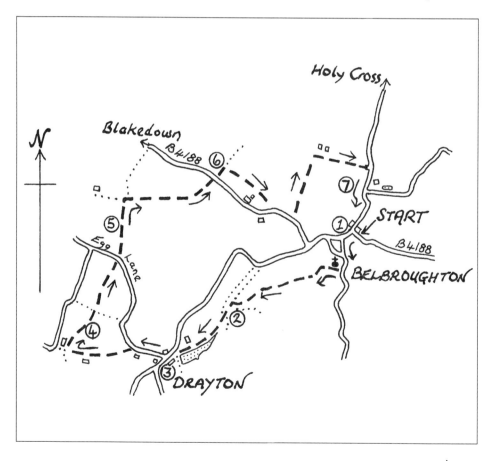

PLACES of INTEREST

The **Clent Hills Country Park** is but a brace of miles to the north, with much lovely walking and fine views.

over a stile on the left immediately after Otter Bank. After another stile a succession of ponds is seen in the valley to the left. At a waymarked stile, just before a farm, go right, with a fence to your left.

❹ After the next stile continue across a field, to again pick up a hedge on the left. Ignore a crossing path. Pass through a gateway, then cross Egg Lane.

❺ The path becomes a track, the hedge switching from your left to the right. At the point the track bends sharply left

instead go right. A waymark post soon indicates the path across a field, slightly left of straight ahead. After the next stile continue on the same line to a stile leading to a footbridge. Carry on from here to a stile onto the road.

❻ Go up the hedged path ahead, then cross a stile on the right. Carry on over a stile on the rise ahead, then after about 200 yards bend right to return to the road. Go left, and left again on a bridleway which leads off a blind bend. The track degenerates, turns sharply right and improves. At the road go right.

❼ Ram Alley Bridge makes a pleasant picnic spot. Return along the road to the village green, between the rival attractions of the Talbot and Ye Olde Horseshoe.

HOPWOOD

Length: 4½ miles

Getting there: Hopwood is on the A441 about a mile from junction 2 of the M42 (signed 'Birmingham South').	**Parking:** On the village street by the post office and also the Hopwood House pub, so long as you patronise it before or after the walk.	**Map:** OS Landranger 139 Birmingham and surrounding areas (GR 031749).

Up in those northern parts of Worcestershire which nudge towards the sprawling mass which is Birmingham there is still much good walking. Many know of the Clent and Lickey Hills, but there is a great deal more. This is an example, leading from the hamlet of Hopwood, which clings to its rural heritage despite the attempted depredations of new roads and housing. One early intrusion is now its greatest asset, the Birmingham and Worcester Canal, these days transformed into a route for that most gentle of boating activities, narrow boats. Higher up the hill Southam's Hopwood Brewery is now no more, but has left its legacy in the shape of an attractive village hall which was once a mineral bottling plant. And then there are the sheltered precincts of Hopwood Dingle, in the careful hands of the National Trust.

Our walk follows the canal towpath north, to the portal of the dark West Hill tunnel, then onto the hill itself. From here the North Worcestershire Path waymarks are a guide through countryside with views out over the plain below. Descending through pleasant farming country, it is pleasing to note how well local walkers take understandable pride in maintaining stiles and gates hereabouts.

THE WALK

❶ The front of the pub overlooks the canal, and steps lead down to the towpath. Go right, under the road bridge, then pass beneath an old red brick bridge. These older bridges have far more character than the modern road bridges, especially when they are mirrored in the still water. The canal enters a serenely wooded cutting, passing under a particularly elegant arched bridge. Then, the dank entrance to the West Hill tunnel is approached. At over 1½ miles it is one of the longest still in active use in this country. The towpath now rises away from the canal, to the road.

❷ Go left along the road. If conditions are very wet you may prefer to stay with the hard surface, otherwise cross a stile at a footpath sign on the left and head up the field. If the path is not clear underfoot, the stile leaving the field is only about 20 yards away from the road at the top of the field, but in the meantime the road has taken a loop. Continue with the hedge to your right to go over a stile on that side. Cross the field to rejoin the road, which has again taken a detour. Go left again.

❸ Pass the entrance to West Hills House and then cross a stile on the right. The footpath sign bears the distinctive pine cone insignia of the North Worcestershire Path, which runs between Kingsford Country Park near Kinver and Major's Green, Shirley. You may catch a glimpse, a little along the road, of the University observatory. Keep to the right of the field and two more stiles lead into a belt of woodland on a metalled path.

❹ Leave this path at the point it curves

PLACES of INTEREST

The **Heart of England Transport Museum** at nearby Wythall houses lorries, buses and rolling stock to evoke nostalgia of days gone by.

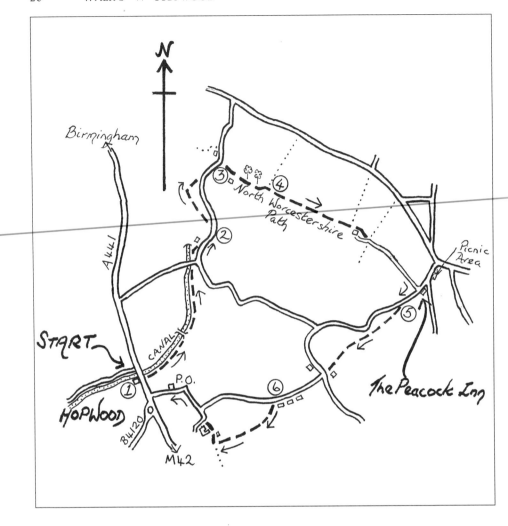

left, by a stile, still with the NWP way-mark. Follow the field edge over two more stiles to pick up a farm track. A waymark post quickly points out a stile, enabling the farmyard to be bypassed on the left. The duck pond will no doubt be fre-quented by a gaggle of mallard. Once past the farm go half right to a stile onto a lane. Go left and soon the rear of the Peacock Inn comes into sight, a very pleasant spot

for half-time refreshments, but our route goes right at the road.

❺ As the road starts to lose height cross a stile into woodland on the left. The path takes a ridge between disused quarries, with graceful beech trees forming a canopy above. On leaving the wood go down the edge of the field to the right. The second stile now crossed is almost superfluous, but

The University observatory glimpsed on the route.

don't be tempted back onto the road. Carry on ahead, with the hedge to the right. After another stile cross the field to another one. Now bear left, along the side of a belt of woodland on the left, to come to the road. Go left and immediately right, down a narrow road.

6 After passing a few houses cross a stile by a gate on the left. Bear half right to a stile in the hedge, then along the left of a field. Cross a stream by a plank footbridge and keep to the left of the rugby field (especially if a match is in progress!). On meeting a lane go right, keeping right through a farmyard to a minor road. Go right. The road curves left to bring you back into Hopwood, with the Hopwood House close by on the main road.

TARDEBIGGE

Length: 3¼ miles

Getting there: Tardebigge is on the B4184, close to its junction with the B4096 (Redditch to Lickey End), about 1½ miles north-west of Redditch.	**Parking:** There is a car park available for public use by the church.	**Map:** OS Landranger 139 Birmingham and surrounding areas (GR 996691).

Some might quibble that Tardebigge is not really a village, only a hamlet. Well, it has a splendidly sited church, a lively school, an impressive pub, and it is picturesquely located with many visitors, so it seems admirably qualified for inclusion in this book. The nucleus is New Wharf, which lies at the point the Worcester and Birmingham Canal completes a rise through a sequence of no less than 58 locks to enter the dark recesses of the 580 yards Tardebigge tunnel. The scene around the wharf is enlivened by the activity and bright colours associated with a narrow boat base. The church meanwhile maintains its spiritual dignity by presiding over

FOOD and DRINK

The Tardebigge was built in 1911 to serve as a village hall for this scattered community. This went beyond the activities we now tend to associate with such institutions, including a library and facilities for a weekly bath (at a cost of 1 penny). Alas, those facilities are no longer available, but this extremely spacious family pub does have a 'Wacky Warehouse' for the amusement of younger family members. The wide range of beers include Calders and Tetleys. At lunchtimes jacket potatoes and filled baguettes are popular and sustaining. If you fancy something that is a mouthful in more than one sense, how about tortellini ricotta followed by capuccino cookie crumble cheesecake? From the church car park return to the B4184 and turn right. Swiftly bear left, under the dual carriageway and the pub is there on the right. Telephone: 01527 550050.

the temporal world from a nearby hill.

The walk itself starts from the church, with distant views to the Clent, Clee and Malvern Hills. The church is dedicated to St Bartholomew, and was built in 1777, although there has been a church here since 1138. Once upon a time it straddled the county boundary between Worcestershire and Warwickshire, but this area is now entirely Worcestershire's. The tower has Baroque elements, but it is the tall needle spire which so conspicuously identifies it in views from miles around. Within, the extravagantly worded memorial to Lady Mary Cookes and her husband is a reminder of a very different age. From here a quiet road and a lane lead to the

Tardebigge Top Lock, the deepest narrow lock in the country.

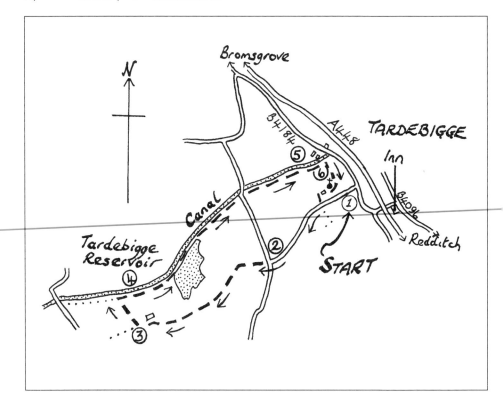

canal. The walk now follows the towpath, by lock and bridge, and the banks of a reservoir, to New Wharf. All along here there is likely to be considerable activity as boats pause or traverse the locks. A final short climb returns to the church.

THE WALK

❶ Enter the churchyard. The church is kept locked but there are superb views over the surrounding countryside. In the churchyard is a wild flower conservation area and memorials to the Earls of Plymouth who lived at nearby Hewell Grange, now a penal establishment for young offenders. Continue past the flagpole and the school. Turn left by a

corrugated iron shed, walking along the edge of the playground and the playing field to a stile onto a minor road. Go right, along the road.

❷ Follow the minor road to the point at which London Lane branches off to the right. At this junction go through the facing gate, which bears a discreet blue waymark. Follow the track for about ½ mile, losing height to approach Patchetts Farm. Pass in front of the farm, through a gate.

❸ Just after the farm buildings go through a gate on the right at a footpath signpost. Cross the field to a stile, leading to a plank footbridge. From here bear left along the field edge to arrive at the canal. Go right. The canal runs from the Gas Street Basin in Birmingham and was completed in 1815. No doubt salt and chemicals were prime cargo, and at one time trade continued right through the night. The last commercial cargo passed this way in 1961, but nowadays pleasure craft make it a lively scene once more.

❹ Now simply follow the canal, passing about half the 58 locks which bargees must negotiate along this stretch. This is the most heavily locked canal in Britain, rising 448 ft in 15 miles. The flight from Tardebigge Bottom Lock to the Top Lock is, at 30 locks, the longest flight in Britain. After a bridge a slight detour up the banks of the Tardebigge Reservoir may be made for a view over this large artificial lake. It was dug for clay to line the canal and to provide water to top it up.

PLACES of INTEREST

The Forge Mill Needle Museum is just north of Redditch and stresses that it is not as boring as it sounds! There are relics of needle-making and fishing hook manufacturing days, and frequent exhibitions. It is set in lovely parkland adjacent to the **Bordesley Abbey Visitor Centre**.

---

❺ Tardebigge Top Lock is the deepest narrow lock in the country, at a dizzy 14 ft. To visit the hamlet of New Wharf continue to the road and turn left. Enter the hamlet by the sign for the British Waterways office. Often boats are being worked on in the wharf. From here the canal enters a tunnel. When you can tear yourself away, retrace your steps to the road.

❻ Returning along the canal towpath, go left through a kissing gate opposite the hamlet. Bear right, the path becoming railed, returning to the car park by the church.

ASTLEY

Length: 5¼ miles

Getting there: At Holt Heath 6 miles north of Worcester turn off the A443 onto the B4196 for Stourport. After a further 4 miles turn left, signed for Astley church.

Parking: There is a car park at Astley church – please do not obstruct any worshippers.

Map: OS Landranger 150 Worcester and The Malverns (GR 787676).

Astley is another one of those villages scattered around the countryside, where the bonds that tie it together are not immediately apparent on the ground. The ancient church may justly claim to be at the heart of this community, although the original Saxon building has vanished without trace. Parts of its Norman successor survive, including the Priors Well, to be found in the churchyard, a reminder that monks once dwelt here. Inside the church, the Blount tombs of 1577 impress by their detail and lively colouration in what is thought to be the original scheme.

FOOD and DRINK

The Hampstall Inn is separated from the river Severn by only a narrow car park. By this is the willow-hung beer garden. On cooler days visitors can retreat to the conservatory, or the darker recesses of the lounge and bar. Here they will find Greenalls Bitter and Banks's Mild. Substantial sandwiches, particularly those with steak fillings, or burgers are supplemented by more unusual dishes, for example Cotswold lamb and leek pie, whilst vegetarians have their own range of specials, such as ratatouille lasagne. Telephone: 01299 822600.

Outside, by the porch, the corbel table with its array of carved stone masks is a most unusual feature. Just to the west of the church, Astley Mill is deep-set in a damply picturesque location. To the east is Astley Hall, once the home of Prime Minister Stanley Baldwin – it is now a residential home.

The walk leads from the church, through woodland, and by Glasshampton. The original house of 1705 was sadly lost when a workman carelessly knocked out his pipe into wood shavings upon completion of restoration in 1810. What you see is the surviving stable block, now a monastery of the Society of St Francis. Soon woodland is entered, in the congenial company of the Dick Brook, then a turn to the riverside at Astley Burf. Here the Hampstall Inn surveys the placid scene. The return is by field

The stone heads which adorn the outside of the church at Astley.

paths and tracks, with the bonus of some wide-ranging views.

THE WALK

❶ Turn left on leaving the churchyard on an initially tarmac then grassy track. After passing through a gateway and by the cemetery extension you will meet an array of waymarks. Go right (blue arrow) down what becomes a bona fide sunken lane to enter woodland. At a fork turn right to cross the stream by a heavily disguised bridge. Cross the track ahead (in other words don't go through the gates on either side) and climb the slope to a pedestrian gate.

PLACES of INTEREST

Astley Vineyard on Crundles Lane is a working vineyard producing white wines. There is a vineyard trail and a shop. In **Stourport,** just to the north, explore the canal basins, usually alive with narrow boats and other craft. Pleasure craft also ply the river Severn.

---

❷ From the gate head across the field to a gateway. Glasshampton monastery is just to the right, but turn left, downhill, on the track. Pass between a pair of lodge houses and come to the road. Turn left, noting the inscriptions on the bridge, which suggest the power of the brook when in spate. Once over, turn right (signed 'Woodend'),

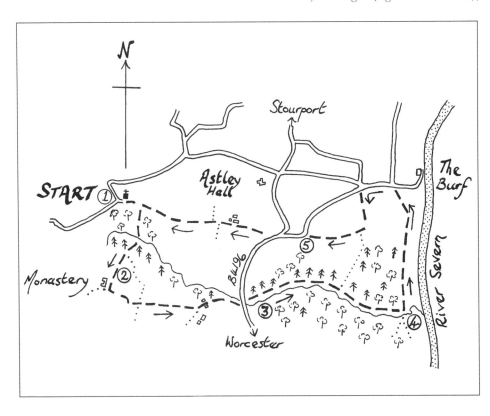

Glasshampton monastery.

but swiftly branch off to continue ahead at a waymarked gate.

❸ Over the field, a sequence of gates follows as woodland is entered. Amongst the variety of trees the sweet chestnut casts its distinctive fruits underfoot in the autumn. Surprisingly, the Dick Brook, which runs alongside, had locks upon it to enable iron-ore bearing craft to navigate it to a forge higher up the valley. These works were probably carried out by Andrew Yarranton, a 17th-century entrepreneur.

❹ The track eventually curves left – keep close by the wood on the track. This will lead you to the road at Astley Burf. The riverside and the Hampstall Inn lie just to the right. Return along the road, passing this point. Bear left at a fork in the road.

After the last bungalow go over a stile on the left. Across the field is a footbridge, then climb the slope to another stile. Go right, on a track, to the road. As you walk along the track, to your right is Astley Vineyard.

❺ At the road go left, to the road junction. Cross over to join the track signed for Solhampton Farm. Astley church, our destination, is now in clear view ahead. Bear to the left of the farm buildings and once past them you will come to a bridleway T-junction. Go right, then leave the bridleway after passing through a gateway and go left (yellow arrow) with the hedge to your left. Go through another gateway and across a field to rejoin the outward route by the new cemetery.

OMBERSLEY

Length : 6½ miles

Getting there: Ombersley lies just to the west of the A449 between Worcester and Kidderminster, about 6 miles from Worcester.	Parking: On the village street, by the church.	Map: OS Landranger 150 Worcester and The Malverns (GR 845635).

Ombersley was born out of its location where springs provided a water supply for weary legionaries on the Roman road. Whilst traces of those days may not remain, it does retain many ornate and interesting black and white cottages, some displaying origins more distinguished than the norm. For example, near the hectic

roundabout at the centre of the village stands Cresswells. If you look carefully at the intricate half-timbering on the end wall you will discern the original oaken crucks that form its basic structure. By the way, autumn is the time to stand here, when the flaming leaves of the ancient chestnut tree distract one's attention from

---

FOOD and DRINK

The Cross Keys Inn is just north of the roundabout, on Main Street. It has a nicely intimate atmosphere generated by beams and arches, enhanced no doubt by offerings of Marston's Pedigree and Timothy Taylor Landlord bitters, plus Red Stripe and Iennents Extra lagers. The standard menu includes mixed grills, omelettes and steaks, and the blackboard might offer delicacies ranging from rack of lamb, through smoked hickory ribs and chicken tikka (all with chips and salad) to smoked haddock and tagliatelle with salad. Telephone: 01905 620588.

---

the frantic traffic. Nearby, the soaring spire of St Andrew's was built in the 1820s. Inside, the church still has box pews and an old stove, but perhaps of more interest are the remains of the old church, which are to be found in the churchyard. Of 13th-century origins, it became the mausoleum of the Sandys family of nearby Ombersley Court. The trees which so well hide the Court from view appropriately include a wellingtonia planted by none other than the Duke of Wellington in 1849.

The walk leads by the Kings Arms, where the future King Charles II is reputed to have slept after the battle of Worcester. From here the Wychavon Way is followed, then field paths, to closely approach the distinctive profile of Westwood House. The core of the house is early 17th century, with diagonal wings added a little later. The roofline is especially exuberant, From here tracks and paths are followed across country, and through the pleasant hamlet of Uphampton, to return to Ombersley.

The Walk

❶ From the roundabout walk down Main Street in the direction of the church of St Andrew. Close by is the Sandys Mausoleum. A little further along the street, on the opposite side, a lane goes off alongside the Kings Arms – there is a guide post if you look closely. As you glance back from the entrance to the lane, on the wall of the house opposite is the original tablet marking its origin as a charity school. The lane becomes a path opposite the last house, which is the cue to branch off to the right (waymarked for the Wychavon Way). The path curves round to some steps down to the A449 – take care crossing as drivers seem perplexed at seeing ramblers! Steps lead up the opposite side.

❷ Cross a stile at the top of the steps and keep to the left of the field to another stile. Cross the field ahead, passing through a gateway to arrive at the edge of a wood. Bear to the right, passing through two gateways. Do not follow the track to the farm through the next gate, instead continue down the edge of the field to join the access track to a house you will pass. At the road go right, cross over, and go down the Hadley road on the left.

❸ The road bends right, but when it bends to the left instead continue ahead

---

PLACES of INTEREST

In Droitwich, east of Ombersley, the **Spa Brine Bath** is unique in Britain. Float, suspended by the buoyancy rivalled only by the Dead Sea. Saunas, massage and a fitness centre should tone you up for your next walk.

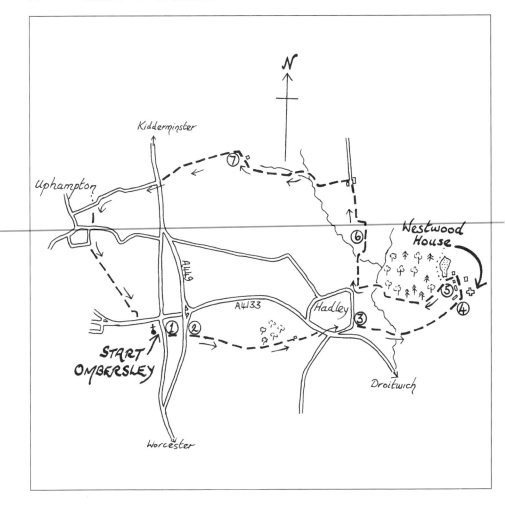

down a lane. This finally passes some
rather derelict farm buildings to arrive at a
gate. Go through, over a bridge, and bear
slightly left over a field. Three stiles follow
in rapid succession, then keep to the left
up a slope to a gate in the top left corner of
the field. From here there are views back
over the countryside as far as the Malvern
Hills. Carry on over the field, bearing
slightly left of the distinctive skyline of
Westwood House.

❹ Meet a track. Facing you is a stile into
a garden. The right of way crosses the
garden diagonally right, alternatively you
could respect their privacy by a slight tres-
pass along the track to the right then left
on the roadway. There are glimpses of the
great house, although the public are
denied a really good view from the footpath here. Don't forget to look left as a
path goes off between First Cottage and
Park View House. Go through three gates

Ombersley.

to the bottom of the field. Glancing over the hedge to the pool on the right I was surprised to see a sinister black bird swimming there – it transpired that it was a cormorant.

❺ Now go left, bisecting the field to come to a gate. You are again following the Wychavon Way, keeping to the right of the field. Do not go through a gateway unless it bears the 'WW' waymark. The path becomes fenced on either side as it leads to the edge of Nunnery Wood. Follow the woodland edge on a clear path, dropping down to the Hadley Brook. The Mill House is set back by the rushing waters of the mill stream. Climb the hill and as the slope eases turn off right on a signed bridleway. This becomes a sunken track, crossing the brook again, to be confronted by a vision of...electricity pylons. Never mind, go through a gate in a dip to the left of the biggest pylon.

❻ Carry on through another gate to join a farm track. Follow this to Southall Farm. Just past the farmhouse squeeze between the garden wall and the field fence and follow the field edge on the left. At the end of the field cross a stile and then immediately pass through the gateway on the right. Descend to the stream and follow this to another stile and a bridge. Once over the stream head for another bridge in the far corner of the field. Now walk down the length of the field, through a gateway to a gate onto a green lane at the side of a farm.

❼ The lane joins a track – go left. After about ½ mile cross the A449 with the Reindeer Inn just to the left. Proceed down the road to Uphampton. Pass the Fruiterers Arms (if you go in, beware the home brew!), Shortly afterwards cross a waymarked stile on the left and follow the field edge over another stile to a minor road. Go right and immediately left up a side road. When this bends sharply right instead continue ahead down a lane. This becomes a tarmac path. Enter a housing estate where you bear left then right to join the main road. On the left is the unmistakable half-timbering of the Dower House. The roundabout at the centre of Ombersley is now just to your left.

HANBURY

Length : 4¼ or 5½ miles

Getting there: Hanbury lies to the east of Droitwich. Approaching from junction 5 of the M5 take the minor road signed for Stoke Works. After ½ mile turn right for Hanbury. Just after passing the sign for Hanbury church turn left at a T-junction, then right on the B4091. The Vernon Arms faces the junction of this road with the B4090.

Parking: On the B4091, just north of the Vernon Arms pub, away from the junction. You may use the pub car park if you patronise it before or after the walk.

Map: OS Landranger 150 Worcester and The Malverns (GR 966630).

Worcestershire villages come in all shapes and forms, not all neatly clustered around a village green. Hanbury village stands on the Salt Way, a Roman road running from Droitwich to Alcester, with its church proudly aloof on a hilltop some 1½ miles to the north and the village school close by. Splendid Hanbury Hall is about 1½ miles north-west from the village. What better than a walk to draw together these varied facets of a far-flung community?

From the Vernon Arms field paths lead you to the church of Our Lady the Virgin, poised to survey the countryside as far as the Malvern Hills. There may once have been ancient British and Roman forts here, and there was certainly a Saxon monastery. The sandstone exterior of the church is late 18th-century, although much of the interior is medieval. There is a fine decorated ceiling and some suitably grand monuments to members of the Vernon family of Hanbury Hall. From the church you can opt for a simple walk out and return through parkland to the distinguished presence of the Hall. Built in 1701 it is now in the ownership of the National Trust. Particular features are the impressive staircase and ceiling paintings on classical themes. The Hall now houses the Watney collection of fine porcelain and

The impressive Hanbury Hall, built in 1701.

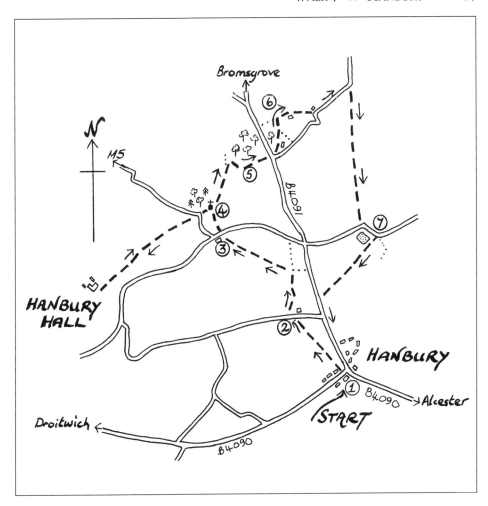

Dutch flower paintings, and is set in 400 acres of parkland and gardens. Whether or not you visit the Hall, the return to the village is through a pleasant mix of woods and fields.

THE WALK

❶ Just left of the Memorial Garden which faces the Vernon Arms is a footpath sign, pointing the way along the side of a house to a stile. Another stile follows, before you go through a gateway on the right and then resume your original direction. This leads up hill to a stile onto a minor road. Go briefly left.

❷ Now go over a stile at a footpath sign on the right. Bear half right to a stile and follow the field edge forward to a plank footbridge into a small plantation. Make for the left-hand fence, where about halfway along is a stile. Cross and keep slightly right over two more stiles and a gateway. The next stile leads through a school car park to a busy road.

❸ Over the road steps lead to a stile and a steep direct ascent to the church. If this seems too demanding, or if detouring to Hanbury Hall, take the road which leads off opposite the school. Just opposite the branch to the church is the entrance to the Hall grounds, identified by a National Trust sign. Simply proceed straight ahead along an avenue of trees and past a couple of ponds. The pay booth is just to the left of the path as the Hall is approached. The return is by the same path and so to climb the road to the churchyard.

❹ Both routes converge in the churchyard, a fine viewpoint over the surrounding countryside. After wandering around and examining the memorials in the church itself make for the far left corner of the churchyard, from whence there is a gentle descent to the left. Go through a kissing gate and then bear right to another kissing gate at the side of a large gate. The track curves right – ignore a signed footpath off to the left at this point. Just before a farm go left at a waymark post.

❺ The path climbs through a leafy stand of beech and oak trees. Another waymark post guides you onwards, to reach the road opposite the Woodgate junction. Set off

> **PLACES of INTEREST**
>
> The **Jinney Ring Craft Centre** lies on the B4091, ½ mile north of the Vernon Arms. There are twelve craft workshops, a craft gallery, shops and a farmhouse kitchen, all housed in old timbered barns.

down this road, but immediately turn left down a track at a footpath sign. Pass some lovely half-timbered and thatched cottages. On meeting a crossing track go right, over a cattle grid (waymarked).

❻ Approach Piper's Hill Farm, but before the farmyard go left through a waymarked gate. On the right is a barn with a wall pierced so as to form a dovecote. Go through another waymarked gate, now keeping left by the hedge to a stile by a gate. This leads to a road, where you go left. Turn right onto a stiled bridleway, overhung by hawthorn bushes. There now follows ¾ mile of easy walking. On reaching another road go left, then right onto a track.

❼ Before striding off down this track, go right, through a kissing gate, passing a fishpond. In the corner a track leads off between the trees. Simply follow this, with the hedge to your right to come to the road, where you turn left. There is a pavement alongside this busy road, which will return you to the Vernon Arms.

FECKENHAM

Length: 5 miles

Getting there: Feckenham is on the B4090, which runs between Droitwich and Alcester. From Redditch take the A441 south and turn right about 3 miles after Crabbs Cross onto the	B4090. Feckenham is a further 3 miles. **Parking:** Turn off the B4090 into the village. There is a public car park signed on the left.	**Map:** OS Landranger 150 Worcester and The Malverns (GR 008615).

If many of Worcestershire's villages are notable for their black and white cottages, then Feckenham is a noble exception. Yes, there is half-timbering to be seen, but the village is distinguished by some rather refined Georgian properties. In the centre of the village is The Square, attractive houses clustered around a tree-set green. At one end is a distinctive white house with arched windows. Believe it or not, this was once a factory, a sharp reminder that needle-making was once the point of this community. Nearby is the church, where charity boards record gifts from the

FOOD and DRINK

The Red Lion is a large pub on the B4090, about 1½ miles out of Feckenham and passed on this walk. It has an extensive car park, a beer garden and a small adventure-type play area. Inside is a skittle alley and a restaurant, whilst in the lounge are some nice high-backed seats. Have a pint of Tetleys – or Calders, Marston's Pedigree or Castlemaine 4X – whilst surveying the blackboard menu. Home-made shepherd's pie, steaks, scampi and ploughman's lunches are all there. Vegetarian dishes are always available, just ask for the day's speciality. Be warned – even a portion of chips might prove to be a meal for two! Telephone: 01527 892188.

wealthy to the poor in those days gone by. One of those benefactors was John Howman, who in the 16th century became the last Abbot of Westminster. King Charles I gave £6 13s 4d from the revenues of the Forest of Feckenham to the village school. Both these gifts are also remembered in the stained glass of the east window. The forest may have long since vanished, but the 8 ft long medieval chest is made from a single tree trunk and is a worthy relic.

From The Square the walk passes the shady old watermill, loud with the noise of rushing water. It continues briefly on an old salt way, before passing into open country under the slopes of Berrow Hill. A short road walk and field paths provide glimpses of ancient Middle Beanhall Farm. The final stretch touches on the margins of Feckenham Wylde Moor, a remnant of once extensive marshland now a nature reserve. Here, in season, you may be treated by the sight of dragonflies being hunted by a hobby.

THE WALK

❶ From the car park proceed to the main street and turn left. A mixture of styles and age of building can be seen, ranging from half-timbered through to Georgian and Regency. Turn left, along The Square, dominated by shady trees. At the far end go right, along Mill Lane.

❷ Soon the reason for the name of the lane becomes apparent. Pass to the right of the Old Mill, with the sound of rushing water from the mill race in your ears. Cross a footbridge and walk up the slope to the right. After about 50 yards turn left along the bridleway signed for the Salt Way and Morton Underhill. The former is a reminder that in the past packhorses laden with salt from Droitwich would have travelled this way.

❸ Shortly cross a stile on the right and climb the slope to another stile. With the hedge now on your right continue over another stile to arrive at a minor road. Cross the road and go through a gate signed for a bridleway. Keep right of the ponds through two gates, then continue above the farm. A hedge will appear on your left, leading you to another gate. The path is now narrowly hedged and fenced, opening out as it traverses the base of a hill. After another gate the slope to the

PLACES of INTEREST

White Cottage Garden at Stock Green, south of Bradley, is a plantsman's garden with adjoining nursery. Particular specialities are hardy geraniums, and there is an interesting stream and bog garden.

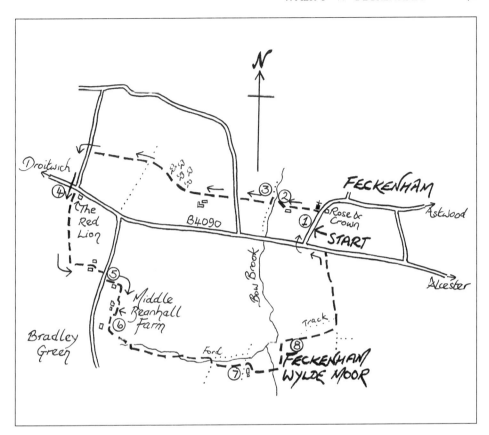

right eases and the path is channelled through two more gates and a belt of woodland. As you emerge the track forks – take the right-hand branch to arrive at another road, where you go left.

❹ At the next junction the Red Lion stands invitingly on the left, but our route continues over the stile facing the junction. Bear across the middle of the field to another stile. Now keep slightly right to a stiled plank footbridge, and then further right to a gateway. From here aim half left to a stile in the field corner, leading into a scrubby area. Go left to a driveway, where you bear right to the road.

❺ At the road turn right and swiftly go left down a driveway at a footpath sign. Keep left of the house, passing through a pedestrian gate and over two stiles. Bear half right to a stile, to find a tennis court ahead. Keep left, around the perimeter of the court. Go over a stile on the left into the field. Now follow the field margin to the right. There are glimpses of Middle Beanhall Farm, which dates from around 1500 with extensions in 1635 and more recently. The brick star-chimneystacks are notable.

The distinctive house in Feckenham that was once a factory making needles.

❻ After passing a small plantation go over a stile in the corner of the field, still with the hedge to your right. At the next stile head diagonally over the field and cross a gated footbridge. Go left and follow the hedge on your left for about ¼ mile. Cross a footbridge on the left (often veiled by foliage during the summer). Once over the stream go right, through a gate. The hedge is now to the right. Pass through another gate, and either cross a bridge on the right or splash through the ford.

❼ Carry on with the stream to the left to the field corner, where there is a bridleway sign. Continue ahead at this point, curving round with a farm to the right. Go through a gate and proceed with the farm to your back. The track bends sharply left, then right. Looking over the field on the right there is a gated footbridge in the far corner. If the path to it is clear, cross the bridge, otherwise stay on the track.

❽ Having crossed the footbridge carry on with the hedge to the left. You are here on the fringe of Feckenham Wylde Moor, a nature reserve, the last remnant of a once much bigger marsh. There is a circular walk (usually muddy) around the reserve, and a bird-watching hide. In the hide is an identification chart to the many species of dragonfly for which the Moor is famous. Our path brings us to Moors Lane, where you turn left to return to Feckenham. At the main road turn left, then right to return to the car park.

HALLOW

Length: 2½ or 5 miles

Getting there: Hallow lies on the A443 Worcester-Tenbury road, just north of the city limits.

Parking: On Church Road or if you patronise the Crown you may use its car park.

Map: OS Landranger 150 Worcester and The Malverns (GR 827582).

Hallow, a holy sounding name, but simply meaning a hill, or rising ground. True enough, the village stands safely above Severn's highest floods. Holiness is emphasised by the imposing bulk of the parish church by the main road, built of local sandstone in 1869. Its 150 ft spire is recognisable for miles around. The heart of this long village is really around the village green. In the 16th-century Queen Eliza-

beth I visited Hallow Park whilst hunting in the area. The house of that name was demolished and rebuilt in 1914, later becoming a school and then a Dr Barnardo's home. Now empty, its grounds are still home to hosts of springtime crocuses and later daffodils.

The walk takes you down to the river, to follow its gently sinuous form, usually in the company of anglers, swans and boats.

FOOD and DRINK

Almost facing the village green, the Crown Inn looks as if it could have served the coaching trade in yesteryear. That feeling grows once you step inside – leaded windows, low beamed ceilings and exposed timbers. It's a big pub, with a separate dining room. The standard menu spans filled baguettes and steaks, with vegetarian and other specials such as grilled salmon on the blackboard. Oh, and desserts such as blackberry and apple crumble. There is a great selection of beers, lagers and ciders, among them Theakston ales. Telephone: 01905 640408.

In due course the river is left behind as you pass through the village of Grimley, where the thatched inn is overlooked by the Norman-founded church. In the churchyard is a very old preaching cross, and the tomb of Samuel White Baker, a now almost forgotten explorer of Victorian times. The way back is past sand and gravel workings. If you want a shorter walk you can leave the river at the Camp Inn to return more directly to Hallow.

THE WALK

❶ Cross the busy A443 opposite the Crown Inn and go right, to the village green. Triangular in shape and shaded by stout trees, pretty cottages surround it. At the far corner Church Road leaves the green – not in the direction of the Victorian replacement church on the main road. More ancient cottages are passed. At the very end go down the signed path. Ignore a stile on the left and then turn right, on a track. There are views over the northern part of Worcester. The track runs down the hill, but about halfway down turn off it on the left at a waymark post.

❷ Cross a stile and continue until you meet the banks of the river Severn, where you turn left. The river, known as Sabrina to the Romans, flows serenely at your shoulder. Soon you will enter the Green Bank arboretum and wildlife sanctuary, a welcome development by a private individual. Carry on until a stile takes you left, round the front of the Camp Inn, no doubt with ducks and peacocks around your feet.

❸ Turn left, up the driveway to the inn. For the shorter walk turn left and meet us again at paragraph 5. Otherwise turn right onto the tarmac lane. Pass a farm on the right, then go down a lane on the right at a footpath sign. On reaching the riverbank again go left, over a stile. To the right is Bevere lock, enabling river traffic to avoid the shallows around the island. Further along the parting of the river by Bevere Island is evident, here amongst pleasant riverside pastures.

❹ The river curves. Boats, swans and fishermen punctuate the view. Look out on the opposite bank for the entry to the Droitwich Canal and the river Salwarpe to swell the river's flow. When confronted by a fence go over a bridge a little to the left. Walk up the lane to the left to enter the

PLACES of INTEREST

In Worcester, visit the **Royal Worcester factory** in Severn Street. Pre-booking of factory tours is advisable; there are also shops and a family restaurant. The **Museum of Local Life** at Tudor House in Friar Street is also very interesting. Here, the way we used to live is displayed in period room settings.

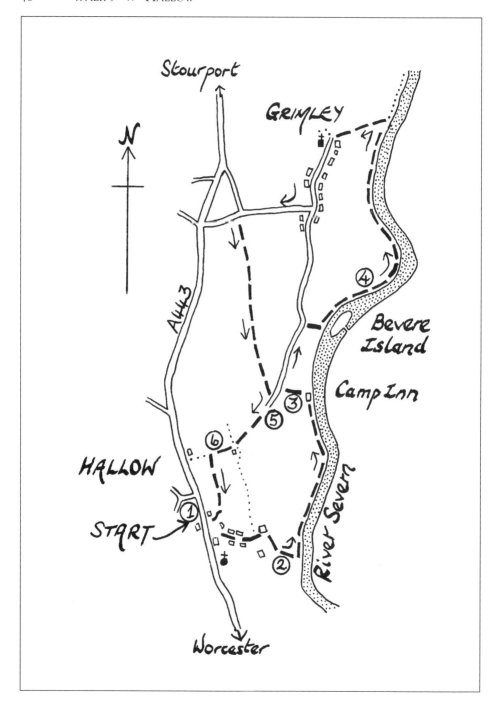

The river Severn.

village of Grimley. One of the first sights is the picturesque thatched Wagon Wheel Inn. Continue along the village street and go right at the junction with Camp Lane. Keep left at a fork and then immediately cross a stile on the left. Follow the field edge over stiles, swapping from one side to the other. On reaching a cobbled lane go right.

❺ Those taking the shorter route will have quickly reached the cobbled lane. This leads to some very ornate gates, also part of the Green Park complex. Our path keeps to the right, becoming cobbled again. At the point the cobbles again end, and the lane swings sharply right, continue ahead at a footpath sign.

❻ The path approaches another stile, but turn left on a well-defined path just before it. Simply follow this path, keeping right where it joins a track, to rediscover Hallow village green. If you arrive on May Day (1st May), you may even find local children dancing around the maypole.

HIMBLETON

Length: 5 miles

Getting there: Turn northwards off the A422 Worcester-Stratford road at Broughton Hackett, about 5 miles east of Worcester. Pass almost through Crowle, and turn right at a T-junction for Himbleton.

Parking: By Himbleton church, taking care not to cause an obstruction if a service is to be held.

Map: OS Landranger 150 Worcester and The Malverns (GR 946587).

Himbleton sits amidst the remnants of the once vast Forest of Feckenham, where the village at one time occupied a clearing. The distinctive weather-boarded church turret is a reminder of those days, and is probably of the 15th-century. Parts of the church are even older, back to Norman days, the font being one example. To the rear of the church is Church Cottage, half-timbered and with a matching dovecote. Down the main street flows the Bow Brook, usually pretty innocuous, but with a reputation for rising rapidly. The resultant floods render the street impass-

FOOD and DRINK

The Galton Arms stands prominently on the village street, although the name on the signboard has changed over the years. Before acquiring its present name it was the Harrow, then the Douglas Galton Arms. The village shop that also used to be housed here has gone too. It has a nice little beer garden, and Theakston ales take pride of place on the bar. Snacks and more substantial meals are available. Telephone: 01905 391672.

able and adjacent houses literally have running water through them. Also on the main road stands the Galton Arms, of which more anon.

The walk leads across fields south of Himbleton to Huddington. Here the Court has been described as the most picturesque house in Worcestershire. Dating from the 16th-century, it has a distinctive tall and ornate chimney in the angle of two wings, but words cannot really do justice to such a characterful house. It also has a story to tell, of treason, no less. Inside is a genuine priest hole, used to hide visiting priests at a time when the Catholic religion practised by the resident Wintour family was outlawed. The discrimination was such that the initial planning of the Gunpowder plot began here, and it was to this haven that the plotters returned after Guy Fawkes was discovered. They then headed north but were captured near Stourbridge and suffered the savage retribution of the monarch. From here more field paths lead to Froxmere Court, and then you continue by woodland edge and good bridleways back to Himbleton.

THE WALK

❶ Return down the street from the church towards the village centre. On meeting the main road turn left (the Galton Arms is just to the right). Turn right down a minor road, with glimpses of quaint, half-timbered Brook House. As the road curves right go over a stile on the left, by the side of the stream.

❷ After the next stile bear slightly right and over two more stiles, passing through a belt of woodland. Cross a field to a plank footbridge and stile. Keep to the left of this next field, passing in front of a farm to a stile in the corner. Through this strip of woodland is another stile, from which you go left to a farm track, turning along it to the right.

❸ Cross the minor road and go down the track ahead. Go through the gates of Huddington Court, not just for a better view of this majestic black and white edifice, but also to enter the church on the left. Please note that Huddington Court is not open to the public and the occupants' privacy should be respected.

❹ Return through the gates and turn right, passing through the farmyard. Go right, through a gate, then left across a field to a stile and a plank footbridge. Now aim towards the far right corner of this

PLACES of INTEREST

Spetchley Park, on the eastern outskirts of Worcester has lovely gardens and trees and is open to the public.

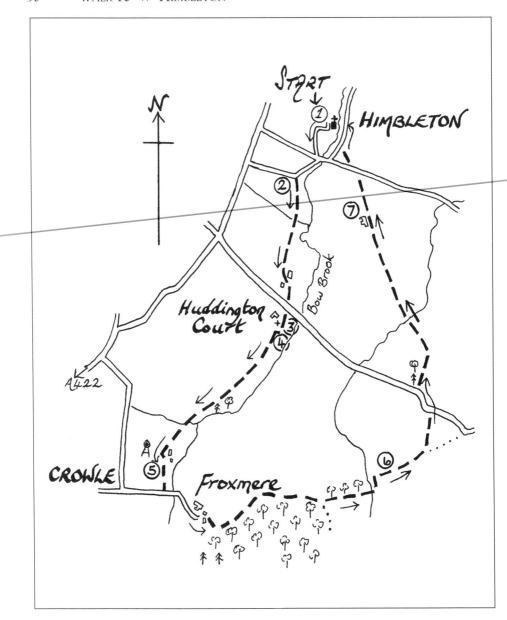

field and from there follow the field edge forward. Cross another plank footbridge, then keep alongside the stream on the left over two more stiles and a footbridge. From here head just right of the red brick gable of a rather dilapidated farm building, well to the left of a wind pump.

Huddington Court, with its distinctive ornate chimney.

❺ Pass through a gate and just beyond the farm cross a stile on the left. Angle across the track to a stile onto a lane. Go left along the lane and pass to the rear of Froxmere Court (note the chimneys) to a gate into a field. Turn right, along the edge of Bow Wood. Carry on through two gates; after the second switch to having a small wood at your left shoulder. Curve left to another gate, then a gateway. Now go left, still along the woodland edge, and at the field corner go right.

❻ Join a track, but when this bends right carry on instead along a path through a rather overgrown green lane. Pass through a small gate. At the road turn left, up a rise. Turn off at the top of the rise along a track on the right. Pass through a gate – don't be deterred if there are some nettles here, the track soon improves and becomes a comfortable companion for a mile.

❼ Pass New House Farm and at the road turn left. Now go along a bridleway on the right, except in wet conditions when it may be better to continue to the road junction. Leave the bridleway and turn right along the road. After about 100 yards turn left over a footbridge to return to the churchyard.

KINGTON

Length: 5 miles

Getting there: Kington is signed off the A422 Worcester-Stratford road east of Worcester, about 9 miles from the city centre.	Parking: By the church – please do not obstruct at times of service.	Map: OS Landranger 150 Worcester and The Malverns (GR 990559).

The rolling countryside east of Worcester conceals many villages, few of which are individually visually outstanding but most of which contain something of interest. Kington and its near neighbours Dormston and Flyford Flavell fall into this category. Kington is notable for the half-timbered tower of St James' church. To the north of the church are earthworks suggesting that there was once a substantial village here, much reduced in medieval times, perhaps by the Black Death.

From Kington the route heads across country, with an opportunity to detour (¼ mile each way, included in the overall distance) to Moat Farm at Dormston. Dated

FOOD and DRINK

At first glance the Boot Inn at Flyford Flavell is a slightly ornate brick built pub of the 19th century. Look more closely and you will see that this fronts the original half-timbered premises. Enter, and through the small front bar is the beamed and timbered lounge and dining room. There is also a super conservatory – and is that a well in the floor? The tempting menu includes lunchtime snacks such as French sticks and ploughman's lunches. For something more elaborate, start with jellied eels and progress to half a braised guinea fowl. There is a children's menu, and in between one for older children or adults with smaller appetites – for example, scampi or steak and kidney pie. The drinks include Bass, Pedigree, Guinness, Heineken and Strongbow and there are wines to complement those intriguing meals. Telephone: 01386 462658.

1663, it is thought to be around 100 years older. The tall gables are distinctive enough, but what sets it apart from others are the tiled weatherings, short roofs protruding from the walls and intended to protect the vulnerable wattle and daub construction from the raw elements. Nearby is a half-timbered dovecote. From close by here the Wychavon Way is joined, running alongside Grafton Wood. This oak woodland is designated as a Site of Special Scientific Interest, but most visitors are likely to be interested by the swathes of springtime bluebells. The route then leads through Flyford Flavell (meaning 'trackway through the forest') and so back to Kington.

THE WALK

❶ Having had a look around the church, return to the main street and go along it to the right. At a footpath sign go right,

between the houses. After crossing a stile bear right, along the field edge. Go through a gate and bear left. At the bottom of the field another stile leads through some damp woodland via a footbridge. Cross a field to a gate onto the A422.

❷ Take care here as traffic travels quickly. Cross to a stile and continue along the field edge. Go through a field gateway on the right at the top of the gradual rise, but then carry on along the same line as before, with the hedge now on your left. Just round the corner at the bottom of the field cross a footbridge. Proceed along the left of this field to a stile onto the road.

❸ Carry on along the road, to the Dormston turn. To see Moat Farm go right at the junction and the farm is about ¼ mile along the road, on the left. Returning to the junction, go right and quickly left along a bridleway, signed 'The Shrubbery'. This becomes a path overhung by bushes. Continue to a gate into a field and go half left, aiming for a prominent willow tree. Just beyond is a stile bearing a Wychavon Way waymark.

❹ Now keep to the woodland edge, over a series of stiles. The Way curves left, then over a stile on the right. The path leads

PLACES of INTEREST

Coneybury Country Centre on the A422 just east of Kington junction is a country store and craft centre with a patio cafe, bird garden and farm and children's play area.

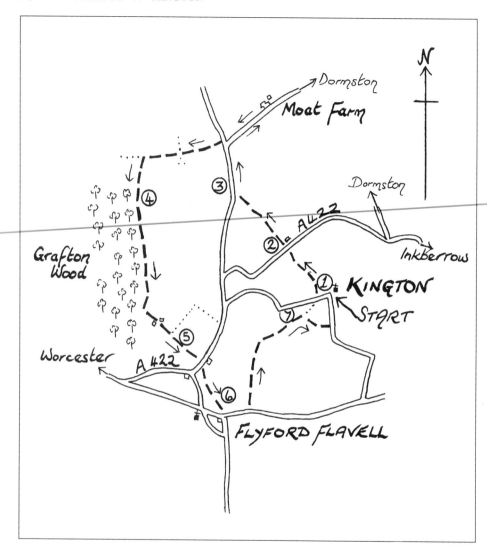

between a house and a barn, down a driveway. When the drive bends sharply left go
right, downhill, with the hedge on your
left.

❺ Cross a stile on the left, then a footbridge on the right, before bearing half left
to a stile enabling the main road to be

crossed. Another stile leads initially right,
then uphill. The field narrows at the top –
escape through the gate ahead. A stile and
a gate now lead into a farmyard.

❻ Go through a gate on the left and then
aim half left to a stile facing the Boot Inn.
Turn left, along the road, and after about

The Boot Inn at Flyford Flavell, a welcome stopping place on the route.

300 yards cross a stile on the left. Continue through a gate to another stile. Another couple of stiles follow, the second just right of straight ahead. Now go right, along the edge of the field, and over a footbridge on the right. Carry on, with the hedge on the left, to a stile.

❼ Angle towards the far left corner of the field, with a gate in sight, but about two-thirds of the way over the field turn 90° to the right to a stile in the corner (this is to accord with the right of way). Bear left along a garden and close by the right of the house facing you to come to the road. Here go left to return to the start.

ALFRICK

Length: 3½ miles

Getting there: Alfrick lies west of Worcester. About 3 miles from the city turn off the A4103 (the Hereford road) at the Bank House roundabout for Leigh. Alfrick is signed about 3 miles along this road.	Parking: There is a layby for a number of cars near the village shop.	Map: OS Landranger 150 Worcester and The Malverns (GR 749531).

The idea that Alfrick might mean elf or fairy kingdom is an appealing, although sadly fanciful, idea. Mind you, Lewis Carroll (of *Alice Through the Looking Glass* fame) was a frequent visitor as his brother was at one time the curate here. What is more, this has been called the most haunted village in Worcestershire, so perhaps one should not disregard these stories. One ghostly couple take their dog for a walk from the old forge to the church. St Mary Magdalene's has a Norman origin and a textbook progression of window styles. There are some panels of

FOOD and DRINK

The Swan Inn in Alfrick is a simple, two-room country pub. The lounge is comfortable and there is a popular bar where the locals meet to exchange news and views. Marston's is available here, and a simple snack. Telephone: 01886 832245. If you are looking for a more elaborate meal go up the road a mile to the Fox and Hounds at Lulsley, which has a lovely beer garden and an extensive menu. Telephone: 01886 821228.

glass from the Netherlands, and amongst the artefacts removed from the redundant church at nearby Lulsley is a 12th-century stone relief of a man with arms akimbo.

From Clay Green at the centre of the village the walk gradually descends to the pleasant environs of the Leigh Brook. Soon one of Worcestershire's premier nature reserves, the Knapp and Papermill, is entered. Around Knapp House is an old apple orchard and woodland, leading to Papermill meadow. There may be a fleeting glimpse of the halcyon kingfisher on the brook, or the shadowy shape of a brown trout in the water. The walk returns through quiet, rolling countryside and by the church.

THE WALK

❶ From Clay Green walk along the main road towards Leigh, passing the Swan Inn, built in front of what was presumably the

Pivany Bridge.

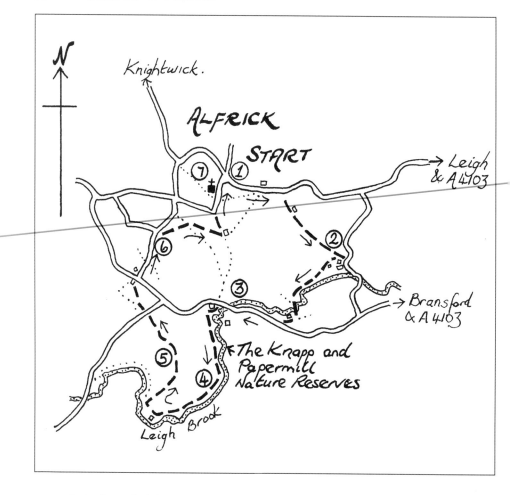

original ale (or cider) house. Opposite is the pond, a mite too small for swans. Up the rise go right on a tarmac track at a footpath sign. Keep right of Luckhold Farm, which has an unusual viewing tower, on a grassy trod. At a waymark go slightly left into a field, hedge to right.

❷ Pass through a gate. Now, the right of way heads to the road, then doubles back to the gate below you, in the bottom corner of the field. Through this gate, keep

some old buildings to your left, then make for the banks of the Leigh Brook. After a plank footbridge and a stile cross the brook

PLACES of INTEREST

Just north of Alfrick is the privately-owned nature reserve of **Ravenshill**. There is a visitor centre and a look-out tower. In the direction of Leigh is the ancient **tithe barn**, the largest timber framed one in the country. It is now protected by the National Trust.

on a heavy duty footbridge by a smart thatched cottage. Pass in front of the cottage over a couple of stiles, then cross a field to a stile onto the road. Go right.

❸ On the left is the mill, which harnessed the power of the brook until 1973. After crossing the brook enter the Knapp and Papermill Nature Reserves, noting the rich red sandstone cutting at the roadside. The information centre is in the porch of the warden's house, where guides, including one to the nature trail, can be purchased. The path descends through old orchards and by the weir.

❹ The old bridge passed is Pivany Bridge, because the rent on the adjoining meadow was paid on Epiphany Day. Further along, comfrey is prevalent. Climb out of the wooded area by a stile and pass Papermill Cottage. Gunwick Mill used to stand alongside but a flood in 1852 washed most of its remains away. At the field corner turn right, uphill, at a waymark. At marker 11 turn right, at a number 12 turn left, to enter Tor Coppice by a stile.

❺ At a T-junction of paths there is a waymark on a low post. This is the point to leave the nature trail and go left. Keep towards the edge of the wood to pick up a track off to the left. This becomes a sunken lane, leading to the road. Here go left, then immediately right through a gate by a footpath sign. Pass through another gate, then the second of two gates on the right. Proceed with the hedge on your right to the road. Go right to the junction, at which you turn left.

❻ There are some nice houses down here, notably Bewells. When a minor road joins from the left turn right through a pedestrian gate. Follow the fence downhill, changing to the opposite side halfway down. Cross a footbridge and follow the hedge uphill. At the top of the slope aim towards a gate in front of the barn ahead. Once through go down the lane to your left, and at the road turn right.

❼ Pass the church of St Mary Magdalene, with its sundial on the shingled tower. The windows range from Norman to 15th century and have been reglazed with handmade glass and fragments, largely from Flemish churches. The Norman font and other items in the transept were rescued from Lulsley. From the church it is a short stride back to Clay Green.

CALLOW END

Length : 4½ miles

Getting there: Turn off the A449 Worcester-Malvern road at Powick, south of Worcester, taking the B4424 in the direction of Upton to reach Callow End.	**Parking:** At the village hall, unless it is in use, in which case park on Lower Ferry Lane.	**Map:** OS Landranger 150 Worcester and The Malverns (GR 835496).

Callow End it may be now, but once this was Stanbrook, which is where the Abbey stands. Benedictine nuns fleeing the French Revolution moved here and evidently prospered. Pugin the Younger (son of the architect of the Houses of Parliament) designed the substantial new monastery in 1878. This was preceded by the distinctive church tower with its striped bell tower. Distinctive also in that the clock strikes every 7½ minutes, and there are further bells to call the nuns to worship through the day. In the village itself are many traditional black and white cottages, one displaying the ancient cruck form of construction.

FOOD and DRINK

The Old Bush is set back from the main road down a short lane just south of the start point. It boasts a flowery beer garden and a play area with swings and small football goals. Inside it is bigger than it looks from outside, with an open display of structural timbers and a particularly pleasant dining area overlooking the garden. The selection of rolls is extensive and fish dishes such as cod mornay and salmon darne supplement the usual steaks. Children's favourites and blackboard specials are to be found. Marston's Bitter, Pedigree and Oyster Stout are on draught, with a good selection of ciders. Telephone: 01905 830792.

From the village the walk leads out to Deblin's Green, with the distinctive pro-file of the Malvern Hills as a backdrop. The return is by way of Old Hills, open hills which nevertheless grant a panorama over many a mile.

THE WALK

❶ Cross the road from the village hall and go over a stile, passing in front of Glebe Cottage – cruck construction and thatched. At the next stile head diagonally right over a large field with views of the monastery. On reaching a minor road go left.

❷ Ahead is a stile leading onto an old sunken lane. At the end keep left of a black and white cottage on a track, then

Stanbrook Abbey.

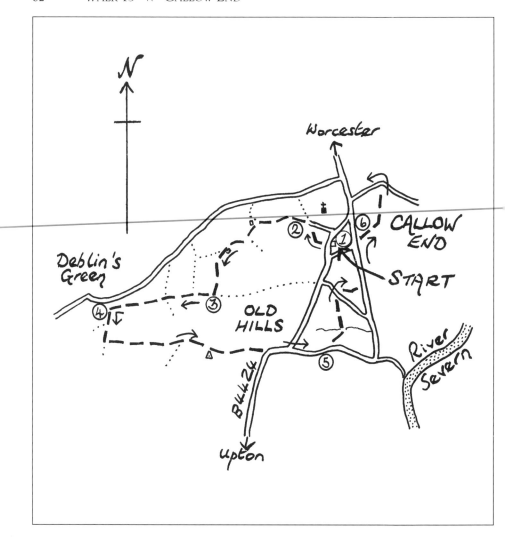

keep to the right of Mount Henwick on a diverted path. Leaving this at a stile, now keep the hedge to your left, passing through a gateway to a stile, faced by common land. Here go right.

❸ Don't go through the next facing gate, but over a stile to the left. Follow the field side parallel to the lane on the right over two fields, leaving by a stile on the right. This is Deblin's Green, which is particularly pretty when the spring flowers are in bloom. Bear left, through the gate for Bryn Derwyn, and just left of ahead a fenced path leads along the field edge to a lane.

❹ Go left along the track. Turn left through a gateway bearing a blue (bridleway) waymark. Pass through a gateway, continuing ahead to the gate onto Old Hills. Ignore crossing tracks to arrive at the triangulation column. Nearby is a seat to relax and admire those wide-ranging views. From here follow the same line to meet the main road at the Pixham junction. Go down the minor road.

❺ At a bend in the road cross a stile on the left. Head diagonally down the slope to the right to a footbridge. Climb the slope, crossing a stile. On the right is Priors Court, where Charles I probably sheltered after the battle of Naseby. Carry on ahead to join a path between the houses. Go left at the road then immediately right down a track which becomes a path, with a stream alongside. At the road turn left, along Lower Ferry Lane.

❻ Cross a stile on the right and head diagonally over the football field (a diversion may be prudent if a match is in progress). Cross a stile, and follow the same line to a waymarked gateway. Here go left on the path to the road. This is Beauchamp Lane, leading to Beauchamp Court, which has been in the hands of the eponymous family for nearly 900 years. Nearby stands The Thatchings, dating from 1450, but we go left, to the main road. The village hall is just to the left.

KEMPSEY

Length: 5 miles

Getting there: Kempsey lies on the A38 Worcester-Tewkesbury road about 4 miles south of the city centre.	**Parking:** On the street, by the church.	**Map:** OS Landranger 150 Worcester and The Malverns (GR 848491).

Kempsey lays claim to being the oldest village in the county, taking its name from a Saxon chieftain called Kemeys. There was an Iron Age settlement here, and Celts, Romans and Normans have all been here since, so you are in good company. St Mary's church, near the start of the walk, has a 13th-century chancel with some nice stained glass in the side windows that is only slightly more recent. There is a little watersplash just outside the churchyard. Cromwell's troops used Cobblers Cottage in Church Street, and it was later the village laundry. The marks on the church tower are said to be due to those troops using it for target practice.

From the church Lanes End leads to the river, where once there was a ferry.

The Severn Way is joined, running along-side the quiet river, with views over to the Malvern Hills. As you leave the water, the imposing mansion known as The Nash is close by. This first saw life around the time of Henry VIII, although it has been much altered since. In the early part of the year colourful displays of spring flowers from snowdrops to bluebells can be seen in the grounds. By way of contrast Kempsey Common is sheep-shorn, other than the intransigent but bright gorse, and provides wide-ranging views before you return through the hamlet of Napleton.

THE WALK

❶ From the church take Lanes End to the river, where you cross a stile on the left and follow the bank of the Severn. The waymarks indicate that you are here following the Severn Way. On the river you

The imposing mansion known as The Nash.

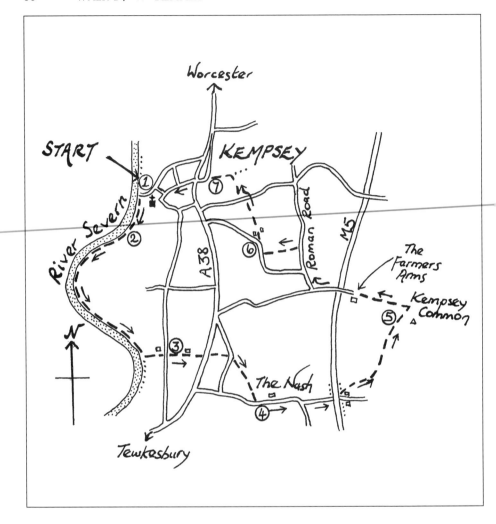

are likely to see swans and frequent plea-sure craft, with views beyond to the Malvern Hills. Deviate a little to the left to cross the Hatfield Brook by means of a bridge before reverting to the river bank.

❷ At the next stile the footpath officially moves even closer to the river, but it is usually more comfortable (and safer) to stay on top of the bank. Enter a scrubby

area, where once stood a bargees' pub, and

PLACES of INTEREST

Upton-upon-Severn, to the south of Kempsey, is a lovely riverside town, with the Information Centre in the intriguing Pepperpot. From here trips on pleasure craft up and down the river place a different perspective on things.

at a waymark post go up the steps on the left. A clear footpath now aims straight across the field to just right of a farmhouse.

❸ Cross a minor road to follow a track to the main road. Take care crossing and just to the left is a footpath sign and stile. If the latter is overgrown there is a gateway about 50 yards to the left. Follow the hedge on your right to reach a tarmac lane. Almost opposite is a field entrance with a path running along the hedge diagonally right. Continue ahead at the point the hedge angles sharply left. A stile leads into parkland, where you must aim about 30° left of straight ahead to a stile to the road. Go left.

❹ On your left is The Nash, fronted by a topiary hedge. Walk carefully round a sharp bend, then turn left down a lane. Pass under the M5 and go through a pedestrian gate by a bridleway sign facing you on the left (not the bridleway which runs alongside the motorway). Now on common land, the path runs beneath trees often alive with scurrying squirrels. At a fence continue to the left until the fence bends right. Now switch to one which has crept towards you from the left.

❺ Here on Kempsey Common there are fine views over to Worcester, with the cathedral prominent, and on to the Abberley Hills. Turn left down a clear track which passes the Farmers Arms. Cross the M5 and turn right at a road junction, now on the line of a Roman road. Ignore a road to the left, pass Napleton Farm, and go left at a footpath sign. A stile leads to a lane, where you go left.

❻ On joining a road go briefly right, and at a left bend leave the road on a track straight ahead. After passing a bungalow continue across a field to the road. Here go left, then right between the houses at a footpath sign, along the back of an estate. Cross a metal stile and a stream and bear diagonally left to another stile, where you again go left.

❼ Over another stile you will come to the road by the doctor's surgery. Carry on to cross the main road, walking now on Church Street to return to the churchyard.

CHURCH LENCH

Length: 5 miles

Getting there: Turn south off the A422 Worcester-Stratford road east of Worcester, to reach Radford. Here go south again for the Lenches.

Parking: By the church, unless to do so would obstruct a service, in which case on street.

Map: OS Landranger 150 Worcester and The Malverns (GR 023512).

The Lenches – a satisfying collective name for a group of delectable villages. Ab, Atch, Church, Rous and Sheriffs Lench are all characterful ancient villages and hamlets, many the subject of benefaction from a wealthy landowner who felt that the quality of the built environment should match the picturesque countryside in which they are set. Church Lench has indeed a church, of Norman origins, although much restored in Victorian times. It contains an early 16th-century cope of blue velvet. Over the road the school palpably exudes learning, bearing messages inscribed on stone bands across its front. Elsewhere are typical half-timbered cottages, one delightful specimen being down the street from the school and just along a side street. This is Toy Cottage, once a one-up/one-down which allegedly housed a family of fourteen.

The walk initially follows the Wychavon Way, through Yeald Wood to Rous Lench. This village underwent a complete transformation at the hands of the Reverend Chafy from 1876 onwards. In the village itself, clustered around a perfect green, are fanciful architectural creations of the Victorian era. This even extends to a half-timbered letterbox! The church displays 12th-century ancestry, and through parkland is seen Rous Lench Court. Massive it may be, but this is a reduced 1840s version of a black and white mansion that stood here from the 16th century. From here good tracks through this wooded, rolling countryside tread the actual county boundary with neighbouring Warwickshire, before field paths bring us back to our start.

THE WALK

❶ Take the track at the side of the church; it bears signs for a public footpath and the village hall. The track splits, with the village hall to the left, just before a gateway. Immediately after the gateway go over a stile on the left and cross to the diagonally opposite side of the field. The waymark on a stile by the gate in the corner confirms that you are on the Wychavon Way.

❷ Continue with the field edge to your right. There are nice views over the rolling countryside. Curve left, then go over a stile on the right, downhill along the edge of a motor cycle scrambling track. Go through a gateway on the left, simply switching from having the hedge on your left to it being on your right. Cross a footbridge and go uphill.

❸ A stile leads into woodland, the path through remaining well waymarked for the Wychavon Way. The woodland is mixed, largely with conifers on the left, but with beeches at one point on the right. After climbing the path falls more steeply. On leaving the wood continue straight ahead, across the slope. Cross a stile to join a narrow, fenced path. At a gate go through a kissing gate on the right, but then simply walk parallel to the track on the left before joining the track and continuing to the road.

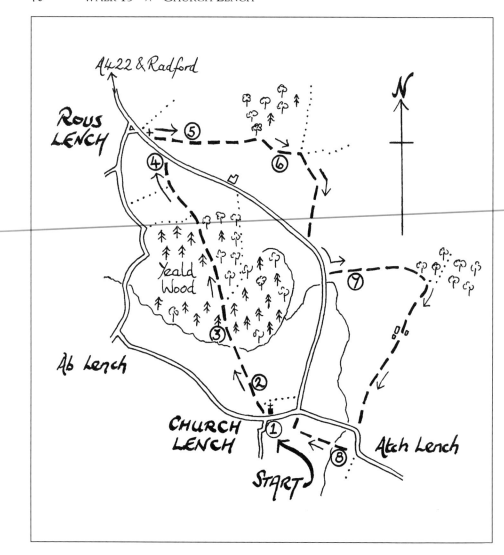

4 Go left at the road, which leads into Rous Lench. The village green is most picturesque, with tall trees, a seat and a half-timbered pillar box. Around are Victorian pattern book houses, one with a well and another displaying topiary. Return along the street but this time go up steps at a bus shelter with a footpath sign to enter the churchyard. Pass in front of the church (usually locked, but if you can go in, please do). The Norman interior finds a contrast in the Italianate lady chapel with gold mosaic in a skylit apse. Rous memorials and effigies are to be seen in a small mausoleum. Leave the churchyard by a kissing gate.

The half-timbered pillar box to be found in Rous Lench.

❺ Enter parkland, initially with a hedge on your left, then continuing on the same line. Just to the right is The Court. Leave the parkland by a stile just to the left of the walled garden. Climb a short, steep slope to a waymark post, carrying on to a stile. Note the Florentine tower, away to the right, but continue on your original line to another stile at the corner of a wood.

❻ Bear slightly right to the next stile, then downhill to a barn, at this point meeting a bridleway running left to right. Take this track to the right, leading to the road where you go left. Close to the bottom of the hill is a tarmac track, at the side of which is a small gate giving access to the bridleway which is now to be followed.

❼ The bridleway runs alongside the tarmac track, then bends to the right. On meeting another track go right, passing a farm to arrive at a road. Go left to enter Atch Lench. At a sharp left bend go over a stile on the right just before Corner Cottage. Go half right down the field to find a secretive footbridge.

❽ Once over the footbridge and the next stile bear slightly right up the hill and go through a gate in the far right corner of this long field. Continue through some rough ground to a stile onto a track. Go right, passing Toy Cottage. At the road turn left, passing the school to return to the start.

SEVERN STOKE

Length : 6 miles

Getting there: Severn Stoke is on the main Worcester-Tewkesbury road (the A38) about 7 miles south of Worcester.	Parking: By the church but if you are patronising the Rose and Crown you may use their car park.	Map: OS Landranger 150 Worcester and The Malverns (GR 856441).

Severn Stoke seems to have more pubs than houses, no doubt a legacy from coaching days. The village stands a short distance east of that earlier traffic artery, the river Severn, which gives the village its name. On the main road is the Old School House and the Boars Head, whilst the half-timbered Rose and Crown stands back behind a beer garden which gives a passable imitation of a village green. The church has an unusual dedication, to St Denys, and is of Norman origins.

The delight of this walk is that it passes through the landscape around Croome Court, created by Capability Brown. Although it was somewhat neglected, the National Trust is doing a sterling job of reinstatement. First seen overlooking the

FOOD and DRINK

The black and white exterior of the Rose and Crown is truly ancient, dating back to 1490. It will be no surprise that the interior is low beamed, but one modern pillar has a carved woodpecker on it. On cool days you are likely to be welcomed by a roaring log fire, whilst on warmer days children will enjoy that large beer garden with its play equipment. The well-stocked bar offers Tetleys and Ruddles bitters as well as Ansells Bitter and Mild. The menu is displayed on a blackboard – largely traditional pub fare, but well-cooked, tasty and in ample portions. Examples include deep fried haddock, sausage, egg and chips (**big** chips) and ham (off the bone) salad. Telephone: 01905 371249.

route is the round Panorama Tower. After crossing the M5 and passing through the hamlet of High Green you will have views of Croome Court itself, begun in 1751 of Palladian design. The estate started life in the ownership of the Coventry family, and then went through a number of hands, such as religious sects. Religion is represented by the prominently placed church, poised to survey the surrounding countryside. The ridge is followed past other features before you cross farmland to the village of Kinnersley on the return.

THE WALK

❶ From the Rose and Crown turn left onto the main road (north) and then right at the Pirton junction. Leave the road at a footpath sign on the right. Keep left of a swampy pool and carry on to the edge of the wood ahead. Here go right, cross a small stream, and continue left along the edge of the wood. The trees disguise the pond although closer views are afforded by the path just inside the wood.

❷ Leave the woodland edge at a stile. There is a glimpse of the rotunda on Cubs Moor on the hill to the right. The path (not clear underfoot) follows the base of the low valley ahead to come to the road at a gate opposite a lodge house. Go left, then right, crossing the M5. Pass through the hamlet of High Green. At a drive on the right two footpaths leave the road. Take the left-hand one, heading straight over the field with the church glimpsed ahead.

❸ At the far side of the field keep left of a small pool. The path now keeps company with a belt of woodland on the right, climbing the hill. At the top, on meeting a crossing path, go right to the church which is poised to enjoy views to Croome Court and the Severn valley and beyond to the Malvern Hills.

❹ A path runs off at the left side of the church, through the churchyard to the road. Go right. On a sharp bend is the gateway to Croome Court, but we continue ahead, initially along a track. Bear slightly right at a waymark post. Enter a field, keeping left. The path soon takes refuge in a grassy strip between two fields.

PLACES of INTEREST

Dunstall Castle is another impressive Croome estate folly, by the side of the minor road from Earl's Croome, at Dunstall Common. **Besford church**, just east of Croome Court, is truly intriguing. Constructed of ancient timbers, and with a rare rood loft, it contains some notable monuments, such as the 16th-century Harewell tomb.

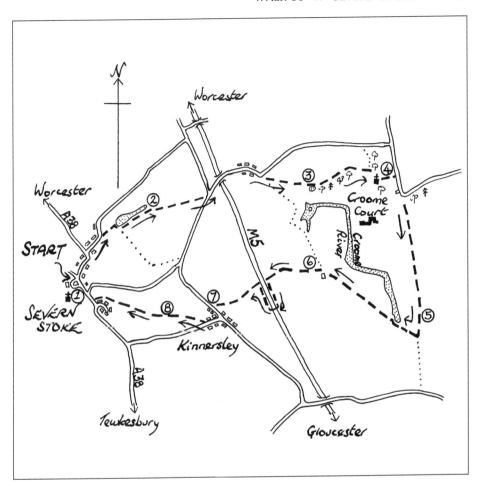

❺ Curve right and then enter the woodland on the left. Just before leaving turn right on the National Trust waymarked path, signed for the Owl House. Past the 'house' descend the slope. At a facing gate bear right over a footbridge and by the side of the Croome River (actually a lake). Leave this pleasantly wooded spot by a stile and diagonally cross the field, aiming just right of the farm now in view.

❻ Cross the farm track, through a gate and then over the fence stile ahead, keeping just right of the wood. At the top of the field cut through the woodland belt on the left and make for the field edge on the right. Cross the motorway bridge and follow the M5 right for a couple of hundred yards. A path then crosses the field to the left, passing through a scrubby area and over another field to the road at Kinnersley.

Panorama Tower.

❼ Go left into Kinnersley, then right at the Royal Oak. Just before leaving the village go through a field gate on the right at a footpath signpost for Madge Hill Road. Bear half left, passing a rather dehydrated pool, to another gate. Carry on, now with the hedge to your left. This climbs to a stile with views of the Malvern Hills ahead.

❽ Now lose height and soon also lose the hedge on the left. A broad, grassy track curves right. At the apex of the garden of the last bungalow on the left, by a double electricity pole, go left along the edge of gardens to the road. Go right and soon the village of Severn Stoke reappears.

OVERBURY

Length : 7 miles

Getting there: From the A435 Evesham-Tewkesbury road turn off for Beckford about 6 miles south of Evesham. Turn left in the village to pass through Conderton to Overbury.	Parking: On a side street, by the church.	Map: OS Landranger 150 Worcester and The Malverns (GR 957374).

Overbury is very much an estate village, in this case as visualised by the Holland-Martin family. This wealthy landowner (of Martins Bank connection) lived at Overbury Court from the 18th century. The Court was built in the classical mould and is harmoniously set in the village. It can be glimpsed from various points, and as a perambulation illustrates the programme of rustication carried out by the architect Norman Shaw in the last years of the 19th-century. One of the best examples of his work is the village hall, where neo-Tudor and Baroque influences converge.

FOOD and DRINK

The Crown Inn at Kemerton, towards the end of the walk, has been pleasantly refurbished, with the stone flagged bar area opening out into the wooden-floored dining area. Bass, Tetleys and Boddingtons are all on offer, but if Sunday lunch is what you seek then please book early – the Crown is deservedly popular. Telephone: 01386 725293.

Of the older houses, Red House is built with Venetian windows. The church of St Faith is set behind a lych gate which is, unusually, the village war memorial. The nave dates back to Norman times, although the most impressive part of the church is the Early English chancel, all vaulting and tracery, with carved bosses and capitals. Have a look at the carvings on the ends of the nave pews.

From the church and the Court the walk leads uphill, through what is a really charming village, largely of stone. Heading in the opposite direction is the stream which once provided motive power for the flour, paper and silk mills. As so often, it is difficult to imagine that now tranquil villages were once bustling hives of activity. Past the village hall parkland is entered, and you climb steadily through woodland to the gentle slopes of Bredon Hill. Magnificent views and a few curiosities are more than ample reward for this gentle exertion. Descent is to Kemerton, which may not possess the individually notable buildings of Overbury but which is nevertheless attractive. The Priory Gardens are open to the public in the summer. From here there is an easy return across the fields to Overbury.

THE WALK

❶ Enter the churchyard through the lych gate, which houses the war memorial. Proceed to the church. On leaving by the porch turn left to go out of the churchyard. On your left there is a glimpse through the ornate wrought iron gates of Overbury Court. Continue around the corner and turn left at the junction. This takes you up the pretty main street of the village. Particularly look out for Red House and the village hall.

❷ As you climb the hill, towards the top look out for the gateway into parkland on the left, and go through to ascend a long driveway. This enters woodland. Upon leaving, at the top of the hill, there is a crossroads of tracks. Go left, with a wall to your left. Go through a gateway and turn right, still on a clear track.

❸ You will come to a wall, over which the steep northern slope of Bredon can be seen falling away. From here there are outstanding views. This is your cue to turn left, still on a track. Soon you will come to the hummocky ground of the Iron Age hill fort, an ideal spot to take a rest and admire the views. From here continue around the

PLACES of INTEREST

At **Bredon**, the 14th-century tithe barn is a massive 140 ft long and is unusual in having the reeve's office on the first floor. The riverside at Bredon is also a very pleasant spot, as the Avon curves close under Bredon Hill. **Conderton Pottery** produces distinctive stoneware in the Old Forge, and you may browse amongst the finished products in the Gallery.

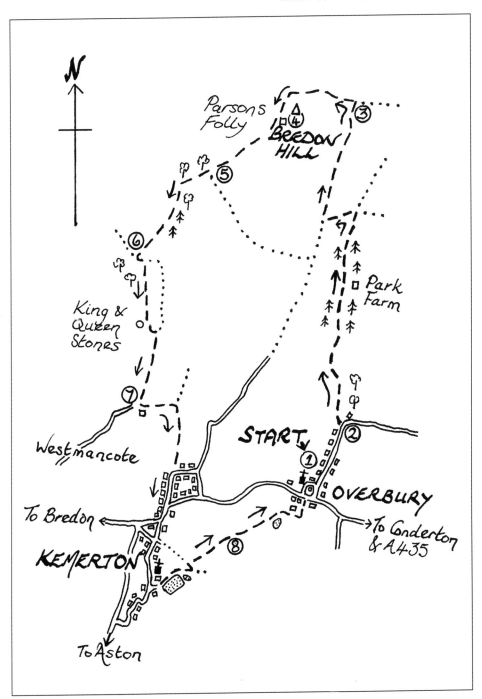

Parsons Folly, allegedly built to raise Bredon to a height of 1,000 ft.

edge of the summit plateau (unless you simply must visit the triangulation column to the left).

❹ Next on this circuit is Parsons Folly, strangely attired with aerials and humming harmonies scarce dreamed of when it was built. The said Mr Parsons allegedly built his folly to raise the height of Bredon to the prestigious 1,000 ft mark. Just below is the Banbury Stone, also known as the Elephant Stone because of the resemblance to that animal from certain angles. Beware, if it should ever hear the chimes of Pershore Abbey, it will rise, to drink of Avon's waters far below.

❺ Soon enter a belt of woodland, ignoring first a path scuttling off to the right, then one signed to the left. Next comes a gate, at which the path angles away to the left, with a small wood on the left. There is another gate, as you start to gently descend.

❻ You will now come to some quarries, with a nature reserve to your left. At this point go left, along a track just above the quarries. Soon there is woodland to the right, and as this comes to an end the King and Queen Stones, once attributed healing properties, can be seen amongst the trees. Another gate follows, after which the track bends sharply downhill.

7 The track becomes tarmacked, which is the point to leave it through a gap in the trees on the left, passing a cottage. Go right on meeting another track, to come to the village of Kemerton. Just continue ahead to the main street and go right then left to the church.

8 A legend surrounds one of the churchyard's memorials. If you touch the middle finger of the outstretched hand of an angelic statue you will have nightmares – it is also rumoured to walk at midnight. On leaving the churchyard go left, then left again, down a track. This passes in front of well-shielded Upper Court, and by a small lake occupied by lively waterfowl to the right. The path leaves the lakeside –

look for a plank footbridge on the left to cross the stream – if you come to a stile you've gone too far! Over the bridge and on a shady track, turn off right after a few yards onto a short track. Go through the gate at the end. Bear right to a gateway in the middle of the hedge ahead. Carry on to a stile and a footbridge, into a small triangular field. Cross the fence on the right and then the one on the left by a sliding pole arrangement. At this point there is a clear view of Overbury Court ahead, but bear slightly right to a gate in the fence on the right. Once through, continue straight ahead to pick up a grassy trod. This bends sharply left to bring you back to the main street of the village.

Kemerton.

ELMLEY CASTLE

Length : 5¼ miles

Getting there: Elmley Castle lies south of the A44 between Pershore and Evesham. If approaching from Pershore fork right on a minor road after the

bridge over the Avon. Pass through Little Comberton to reach the village.

Parking: On the main street.

Map: OS Landranger 150 Worcester and The Malverns (GR 982411).

This is a case of three villages and a hamlet, an opportunity to visit some charming communities in the shadow of Bredon Hill. But some villages have a status beyond their size. Elmley Castle is one such, having been dubbed Worcestershire's prettiest village – not an easy choice with so many outstanding con-

tenders. It has a long main street, with a stream running in a channel alongside, like so many in the nearby Cotswolds. The castle has long vanished, and its history is a matter of some conjecture. It usually features on a display in the church, just one of a number of interesting features. There are two contrasting memorials, that to the

FOOD and DRINK

The mill from which the Old Mill Inn, passed at the end of the walk, takes its name may have long since vanished, but ducks still dabble on the mill pond. Outside the inn are rustic relics, carts and ploughs under the spreading chestnut tree. Inside are handtools and other miscellanea in a comfortable beamed lounge. The French windows to the dining area overlook the cricket field. The menu is no disappointment. The standard offerings are supplemented by a host of splendid blackboard specials, for example a steak and kidney pie served in a rich red wine and Guinness gravy. Moules marinière and cashew nut paella convey the variety, and if you arrive on a Sunday lunchtime you may wish you had booked for the carvery. Bass and Worthington face competition from guest beers such as Ruddles County, and wine buffs will not be disappointed either. Telephone: 01386 710407.

Savage family being of fine alabaster. The Coventry memorial is far more ostentatious, and there is an explanation as to why the first Earl, to whom it is dedicated, is not actually buried here. In the churchyard is a splendid sundial, and all around the village are black and white buildings. Even modern buildings blend in with the overall ambience.

From Elmley Castle paths are followed under the slopes of Bredon Hill to Great Comberton. Close by is Little Comberton, another charming village with many old houses, half-timbering and thatch much in evidence. The old Manor House is surrounded by all the accoutrements of olden-day village life, such as barns, stables, laundry and a bakehouse, many now converted into enviable homes. The tithe barn and a dovecote still remain, as does the church, perched on a mound by the

village pond. The church bears a number of mysteries to ponder upon. Field paths then wend their way through the hamlet of Bricklehampton, with views of an Italianate mansion, on the way back to Elmley Castle.

THE WALK

❶ A visit to the church is a must. As well as those monuments, don't miss the font and the carved rabbit and the pig in the porch. The sundial nearest the path displays a splendid array of gnomons, which achieved a surprising level of accuracy. There is a less ornamented one deeper in the churchyard. On leaving the churchyard pass to the left of the Queens Head on a minor road. The Queen in question was Elizabeth I, who once stayed here.

❷ At the point the road bends through 90° go down the signed footpath on the right. Before crossing a stile by the last farm building go left, along the side of the farmyard. Exit by a farm gate with the field edge on your right. Pass through two more gates with stiles alongside, then climb over a stile on the right. Ahead are views of Bricklehampton Hall. Pass through a gate and go left, along the field side.

❸ After the next stile bear slightly right to another. Two more stiles will bring you

PLACES of INTEREST

Pershore has fine Georgian buildings and a pretty well intact Norman abbey. About 4 miles south of Elmley Castle is **Beckford Silk**, where the screen-printing workshop and shop may be visited.

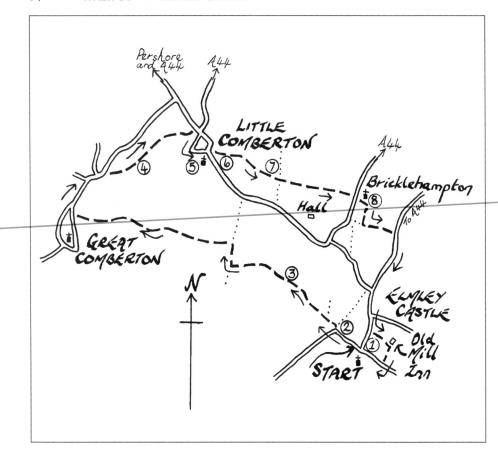

to a track. Go right, then after about 100 yards turn left along a shady but quite distinct track. This becomes a grassy lane which leads unerringly into Great Comberton. At a T-junction go right, then join the main road. Continue past the war memorial, and on the bend after the Pershore junction a footpath sign on the right indicates the line to be taken over a field. If the path is indistinct the footbridge at the other side is by the furthest electricity pole.

❹ Similarly the plank footbridge out of

the next field is by an electricity pole and the lines are followed to the next footbridge. Now head diagonally right across the field to a stile giving access to a passage between the houses. At the road go right along the street of Little Comberton, then right again along Manor Lane. The old Manor House is surrounded by all the necessities of former village life, such as barns, stables, laundry, bakehouse, tithe barn and dovecote most now converted to homes.

❺ Around the corner is St Peter's church,

The charming village of Little Comberton.

believed to stand on the site of a Roman temple. The 12-century nave seems too small for the tower and chancel. Have a look at the stone benches in the porch which were incised with the outlines of the hands of 18th-century brides. Above the door the 11th or 12th-century tympanum is decorated with unusual whorls – are they beehives, clouds or shells?

❻ On leaving the churchyard go right. Just to the left, on the opposite side of the main road, go up some steps and over a stile – the path is signed for Bricklehampton. At the other end of the field the gate is obscured by a massive lime tree. Almost immediately go through another gate and along the length of the field. At the end go over a plank footbridge and stile, then left through a gateway and right along the field edge.

❼ Just around the next corner of the field is another stile on the right. The field edge is initially on the left, but when it bends to the left break away to a stile in the far corner (left of the farmstead). Continue along, with views to Italianate Bricklehampton Hall on the right – looking rather like Osborne House on the Isle of Wight. Over another stile and you will come to a minor road. Here go right then left through the lych gate.

❽ Pass Bricklehampton church, which is kept locked, through the churchyard and turn right. Cross a dirt track and continue ahead to a tarmac lane. Here go left. The lane becomes grassy until a minor road is reached. Follow this to the right to arrive in the village of Elmley Castle. Continue along the village street, then turn left at the sign for the Old Mill Inn. Pass a really nice magpie cottage to find the Old Mill Inn almost at the end of the lane. From here, cross the cricket field to the minor road and go right to the square (take care at the narrowing of the road).

The splendid sundial in the churchyard at Elmley Castle.

WICKHAMFORD

Length: 3½ miles

Getting there: To reach Wick-hamford village, turn off the A44 Evesham-Broadway road about 2 miles south-east of Evesham.	**Parking:** If you patronise the Sandys Arms you may use their car park, otherwise you will probably find a space close by on the street.	**Map:** OS Landranger 150 Worcester and The Malverns (GR 067414).

How do you like your half-timbered houses? Black or white or honey and chocolate? Beetling thatches or pert tile roofs? Sprawling mansion or cute cottage? Blatantly fronting the road or reclusive behind walls and trees? Don't spend too long on these dilemmas, as Wickhamford is one of those rare villages with all types present, a feast for the half-timbering gourmet. Many of these houses are along the street, but set back by the Badsey Brook is The Manor, dating back to the 16th-century, although much of what you can see is less than 100 years old. Of genuine antiquity is the dovecote which can be glimpsed above the garden wall – this was erected in 1214. Next to The Manor is the 13th century church of St John the Baptist. Some of the interior features are of particular interest, such as the box pews with linenfold panels, panelling in the west gallery which came from a London church and fine alabaster monuments to the Sandys family. You can also purchase a copy of the Sandys family tree, showing their connection to George Washington.

From this venerable village it is a short stride to neighbouring Badsey. This has its own magpie buildings, although most housing is much more recent. It has a contrasting Manor House, the Stuart period Stone House, and the engagingly located church of St James. The return is out into

The church of St James, at Badsey.

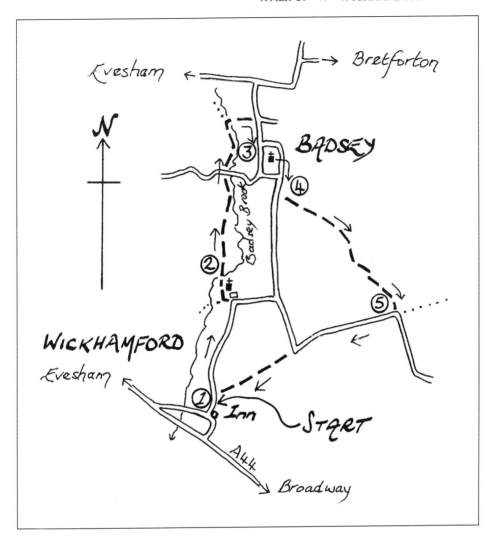

the open market gardening countryside, with views of the Cotswold scarp.

THE WALK

❶ Walk into the village along the main street, admiring the variety of pristine half-timbered houses. Turn left onto Manor Road, with the 13th-century dovecote just visible over the wall. Bear to the right, by The Manor, to the church. There are glimpses of the splendour of The Manor's timbered mass. In the church, there are monuments to the Sandys family, but many visitors will come to satisfy their curiosity about the Washington connection.

❷ On leaving the churchyard go right,

over the babbling Badsey Brook, and continue ahead with the fence to your left. Cross a stile by a concrete chamber, then join a track. Cross a road to join another track, leading by market gardens which always seem busy, whatever the season. Cross the public footbridge on the right (some houses have their own bridges) and then cross an estate road. The path leads to the village street by the side of Badsey's Manor House. This was once the sick house for the monks of Evesham Abbey, and it displays some lively half-timbering. Now go right, along the village street.

❸ The street is a mixture of modern, Victorian and older houses. Turn into St James' churchyard on the left. The church itself is built of honeyed stone, and contains some 17th-century kneeling figures. Much of its charm is in its setting, particularly as you walk past the church to the far end of the churchyard. Here, amongst tall trees, turn and look back to appreciate this. Leave the churchyard at this end and go right.

PLACES of INTEREST

The **Domestic Fowl Trust** is based just east of Badsey at Honeybourne. As many as 160 breeds of hens, ducks, geese, turkeys and bantams are kept in paddocks here. There is also a playground and the Speckled Hen Tea Room.

---

❹ Continue along Willersey Road and then turn left along Sands Lane, which becomes a track. Turn right at a footpath sign, crossing a field to a footbridge. In the far left corner of the field now entered is a stile and another footbridge. Continue ahead with the field edge to your right and Broadway Tower on the Cotswold scarp in view ahead.

❺ At the road turn right. Carry straight on, along a bridleway, when the road bends sharply to the right. This will bring you back to Wickhamford, with the Sandys Arms just to the left.

CHILDSWICKHAM

Length : 4 miles

Getting there: Turn south-west (signed for Childswickham) off the A44 Evesham-Broadway road.	Parking: There is a car park adjacent to the church which may be used if this does not coincide with service times. Otherwise on street, by the inn.	Map: OS Landranger 150 Worcester and The Malverns (GR 075384).

Childswickham has one foot in Evesham's soil and the other on Cotswold stone. As a result black and white, red brick and warm stone are intermingled as you walk around this village. The church is uncompromisingly honey-coloured stone, and the spire can be seen for miles around. It lies a short distance from the green, upon which stands the cross. The top of the 15th-century original was destroyed in the Civil War, so it is now surmounted by an 18th-century urn. Around are calmly elegant houses, the 14th-century Old Manor House being the oldest in the area. Between the church and the cross is the Mill House, no longer

FOOD and DRINK

The Childswickham Arms stands four-square at the crossing of the Hinton, Broadway, Murcot and Buckland roads. This is a genuine country pub, with a beer garden and bar and a lounge where Theakston ales are amongst those on offer. The menu is unpretentious, but whether you order burgers, minted lamb or ham and eggs you will find your choice to be well-cooked and substantial. Telephone: 01386 852461.

in use, but the stream is just one of the appealing features of this village.

From the church the paths to Broadway are by caravan sites and market gardens. Simply stunning is the only way to describe this gem at the foot of the Cotswold scarp, which oozes charm and quality. Allow plenty of time to explore. As a composition it is near perfect, and the components bear detailed inspection – like the exceptional Lygon Arms and Tudor House. From here there is a gradual return to open countryside on the way back to Childswickham.

THE WALK

❶ Start from the front of the church, outside the churchyard. The path crosses a scrubby area and uses stepping stones over a stream. From here bear half right to a

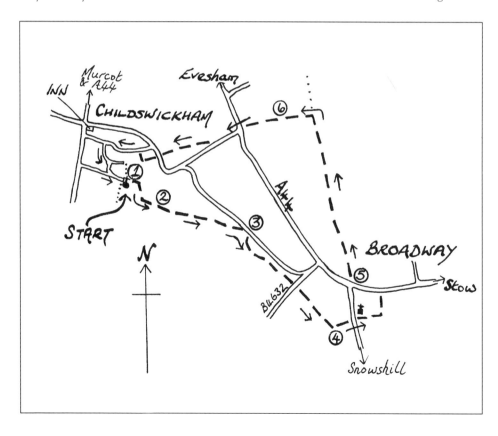

Broadway, perhaps the most famous village in the Cotswolds.

concrete block building. Now go right then left along the next field edge with the hedge on your left. This takes you along the length of a large caravan site. At the far end cross the facing stile and go left.

❷ Cross another stile which takes you through more scrubby grassland, but in autumn elderberry collectors will vote this a treasure house. The next stile leads into a cultivated field, which has to be crossed to the far left corner. After the stile to be found there keep initially right of the stream to a footbridge and so to the road. Go right.

❸ Go under the bridge and immediately right over another stile. Curve left along the field edge by some market gardens. Cross a road, pass along the side of a house and through some neatly tended allotment type gardens. After the next stile follow the field headland to another stile. Keep

---

PLACES of INTEREST

Barnfield Court and Wine Mill on the Broadway road is a cider museum where in season cider and winemaking can be seen. In Broadway there is the **Teddy Bear Museum**, and on Fish Hill the **Broadway Tower Country Park**, centred on the Folly Tower. Around it are animals, an adventure playground and a restaurant.

left to one more stile and a footbridge. From here there is a nice photo opportunity of the warm Cotswold stone house and the church ahead.

❹ Over the footbridge, keep through a kissing gate to the road. The church is to the left if you wish to detour there, otherwise cross the road and head down the facing track. Go through a kissing gate, then left, through the car park and a pleasant shopping arcade to the main street of Broadway.

❺ After looking around this lovely village return to the village green. Opposite the Snowshill junction leave the main street at China Square. Carry on along this road which gradually becomes more and more rural. Cross the disused railway line and carry on ahead. After about 200 yards there is a stile at the side of a gate-

way. Either go over the stile or through the gate and aim half right over the field. Those with keen eyesight will see the waymark post halfway along the facing field boundary. This indicates the position of a stile.

❻ Once over the stile carry on ahead to go through the hedge and bear left up to the main road. Carefully cross over and go down the facing Childswickham road. At the base of the slope go right then left on a rough track, passing between some sheds to arrive back in Childswickham. Cross the road to a lane which narrows to a path. It is worth going down a path on the right then left and left again to go down Twitcham Lane to the cross. From here go left to return to the church. The little circuit takes in many of the original attractive houses in the centre of the village.